Catherine Hills

Blood of the British

From Ice Age to Norman Conquest

George Philip
in association with Channel Four Television Company Limited

The television programmes on which this book is based were produced for Channel Four Television by the Unicorn Organisation Ltd.

British Library Cataloguing in Publication Data

Hills, Catherine
    Blood of the British.
    1. Great Britain—History—To 1066
    I. Title
    941.01   DA135

ISBN 0-540-01102-9

© Catherine Hills 1986

First published by George Philip,
27A Floral Street, London WC2E 9DP

Filmset in Monophoto Ehrhardt by
Tameside Filmsetting Limited, Ashton-under-Lyne, Lancashire
Printed by Butler & Tanner Ltd, Frome, Somerset

ILLUSTRATION ACKNOWLEDGEMENTS

Ashmolean Museum p. 172; Nick Barton p. 18; Bath Archaeological Trust p. 113; J. & C. Bord pp. 44–5, p. 55, p. 61, pp. 62–3, p. 90, p. 98, p. 119, pp. 202–3; British Library p. 219; British Museum p. 77, p. 108, p. 125, p. 126, p. 132, p. 167, p. 200, p. 217, pp. 234–5; Cambridge University Collection of Air Photographs pp. 70–1, p. 151, p. 245; Cambridge University Museum of Archaeology and Anthropology p. 20, p. 21, p. 79, p. 96, p. 97, p. 170; Danebury Trust p. 85; Mike S. Duffy, York Archaeological Trust p. 179, p. 194; G. Eogan p. 57, p. 58; Fitzwilliam Museum, Cambridge p. 103; Andrew Fleming p. 38; Michael Fulford p. 128; Peter Hawes p. 19; Historical Museum, Stockholm p. 196, p. 197; Institut for forhistorisk arkaeologi, Moesgard p. 23; A. F. Kersting p. 53, p. 107, p. 137, p. 225, p. 229, p. 233; Landesmuseum für Vor- und Frühgeschichte, Schleswig-Holstein p. 153, p. 154; P. Mellars p. 22; Martin Millett (drawn by S.T. James) p. 160; Richard Muir p. 157; Christopher Musson pp. 222–3; National Museum of Antiquities of Scotland p. 139; National Museum of Denmark p. 199, p. 211; The National Museum of Wales p. 14; Niedersächsisches Landesinstitut für Marschen- und Wurtenforschung, Wilhelmshaven p. 155; Norfolk Archaeological Units p. 163, pp. 164–5; Photo Georges Gaud p. 214; Photographie Giraudon p. 80; Francis Pryor p. 60, p. 90; Public Record Office: Crown Copyright p. 242; P.A. Rahtz p. 162; Sidney Renow p. 135; Dr P.J. Reynolds, Butser Ancient Farm Project Trust p. 29, p. 100, p. 101; Anna Ritchie p. 188; Warwick Rodwell p. 239, p. 240; The Royal Commission on the Historical Monuments of England p. 230; Mick Sharp p. 41, p. 50, p. 51, pp. 66–7, p. 68, pp. 142–3, pp. 148–9; Society of Antiquaries p. 83; Somerset Levels Project p. 34; George Taylor p. 10, p. 106; Timothy Taylor, MA Cantab p. 24; University of Durham p. 195; University Museum of National Antiquities, Oslo p. 184, p. 185; Derek Widdicombe p. 76, p. 88, p. 111, pp. 114–15, p. 118, pp. 122–3, p. 228, p. 237.

Contents

Introduction

This book is based on the television series *Blood of the British* made by Unicorn for Channel 4 and first shown in 1984. The series was directed by Forbes Taylor, who wrote the first version of the scripts and who was the main impulse behind the series. I have no idea why he thought of me when he was looking for a presenter, since I had never had anything to do with television before – and I was surprised, flattered but sceptical when he sent me his scripts and asked if I would be interested in becoming involved. I felt sure I was not good television material, since I hate having my photograph taken and find it impossible to look straight into the sun without weeping copiously. (We did indeed have a lot of trouble in that direction, but I was only once allowed to retreat behind my sinister sunglasses.) I also suspected some other disaster would strike before we actually got to filming, so I rashly agreed, not thinking it would really happen. But I did make the small proviso that the scripts should be drastically altered, almost turned on their heads in some ways, since my views were often rather different from Forbes'. So we spent many hours, usually quite enjoyably, trying to agree on alternative versions.

Slightly to everyone's surprise we did successfully make the series and people even watched it, at various inconvenient late-night hours. Some of them even wrote to me, mostly very interesting and kind letters for which I am grateful. At times I think Forbes must have wished me back-filled into a deep excavation and I certainly developed doubts about the glamour of life as a television presenter: essentially one is a piece of scenery, to be propped up occasionally to say the next piece when the camera crew have arranged the weather, and otherwise left to try to get on with something else. But I did find it interesting and I did learn a great deal, one way and another.

One reason for agreeing to do the series was that I think there is a gap between professional archaeologists and the public in their view of the past. It sometimes seems as if more and more information is being recovered through new techniques of excavation and analysis, and greater investment of time and money in archaeology, only for it to remain locked up in a few minds and in many archives and museums. The popular idea of the past still depends on endless rehashing of the same old ideas, many of which have been discarded or radically altered by recent research. This is a great pity, since the new versions of the past depend on more information than the old, and are often more interesting. Archaeologists are not trying to create a private past for themselves (at least, most of us aren't). Our findings should be communicated to as wide an audience as possible, as soon as possible. That is not at all easy, since not only are most of us busy, but there is a natural reluctance to boil down quantities of complicated information into eight half-hour television programmes or seven short chapters of a book. Oversimplification can result in distortion through biased selection. But I think that, if an opportunity to reach a wider audience presents itself, as it did to me, it should be taken. If we can communicate to students at nine o'clock on a Monday morning, then Thursday at midnight should be no problem – half the audience will be asleep in either case.

I hope among other things that my prehistorian colleagues will forgive an Anglo-Saxonist for trespassing on their territory. In defence, I can only say that I have found their work very interesting in recent years, looking at it from a non-specialist standpoint, and that I have tried to convey some of that enthusiasm from the position of someone who has, I hope, enough knowledge to see what they are trying to say while yet being far enough away to see the wood for the trees. This is not true for the later chapters, and I hope they have not lost in clarity because I am too close to the detail. In any case, wherever possible I have got people to speak for themselves and to explain their work in their own words. On television they can be seen and heard doing so: in this book I have tried to keep as closely as possible to what was said, and I hope I have not misrepresented anyone.

The series and the book are of course a very small contribution to the bridge between academic and public, and they are also compromises in various ways. In the first place, the scripts were a combination of the ideas Forbes outlined and my own ideas. The original versions concentrated on the successive arrivals of different peoples in Britain, each bringing new ways of life and to a greater or lesser extent destroying what already existed. There was also a concern with ancestry and with the mixture of peoples who have come to make up the present British nation. This is reflected in the title, *Blood of the British*, but the theme of the eventual programmes and of this book is rather different. This is because recent archaeological thinking has turned away from a view of the past which saw all change as the result of invasion, and has concentrated rather on showing how changes developed within societies. New pots and even new kinds of buildings do not always mean new people. Why should the natives never think of anything for themselves? There are of course well-known recorded invasions of Britain, such as those of the Romans, Saxons, Vikings and Normans, and there may have been similar invasions and migrations in the prehistoric past. But to explain all change in such terms is not an explanation at all. In any case, when looked at carefully, those recorded migrations were not always so totally disruptive as has been thought, nor did they leave a straightforward picture in the archaeological record.

It is also not so clear now as it used to seem that peoples or tribes whose names we know from very early historical sources, such as the Celts, were very precisely defined ethnic groups, quite different from other contemporary peoples. Still less can we be sure that an archaeologically definable 'culture', or group of similar material remains, corresponds directly to an ethnic group. It is all much more complicated than that, and much more difficult to summarize, but more interesting. Instead of seeking for the mysterious origins of aggressive conquerors we have to look in a much broader way at the development of society, and see how changes happened for all sorts of reasons, many of them internal. When an invasion did happen, the interesting questions to ask are 'Why were the natives susceptible to attack?' and 'What advantages did the newcomers possess and what real long-term effects did their arrival have?', rather than simply 'Where did they come from?'

In this book I have first tried to outline what we know about the prehistory of Britain since about ten thousand years ago. I have tried, very briefly, to show how much could be explained in terms of the continuing development of society within Britain. There were fluctuations and even dramatic changes from one period to another. Some of these may have been partly caused by incoming people: very often it is more likely that climate, overexploitation of land, the growth or decline of population and shifts in political or social structures were more significant. The first three chapters of the book cover a very long period in a very general way. I then turn to a more detailed consideration of more recent periods, focusing particularly on the times when there have been recorded invasions.

Although to some extent this perpetuates the idea I am trying to criticize, that invasions were always the most crucial reasons for change in the past, what I hope I can show is how strong the degree of continuity was, even after what look at first sight to be complete and devastating conquests. I shall also try to show that, if we did not have historical accounts for the last two thousand years, on the basis of archaeological evidence alone we might very well not suggest that invasions had happened when they did. This is not because the archaeological record is inadequate or wrong: it is partly because we do not always interpret it correctly, and partly because the kinds of human activity best reflected in archaeological evidence are often not

Sometimes it seemed as if the pots were the invaders.

those aspects of life most changed by wars, coups and the rise and fall of ruling cliques. It also reflects the fact that such political changes are sometimes superficial, and do not have fundamental effects on the lives of ordinary people. This makes it all the more important to guard against interpreting prehistory in terms of invasions which, if they did happen, may not have left very obvious traces. Understanding of the past can only come through a holistic approach, in which the internal dynamics of a society and the relationship of man with his environment are given at least as much, if not more, significance as relationships between societies, whether friendly or hostile, equal or unequal.

Another compromise which I could not avoid is that the book is divided chronologically. It is impossible to understand the past without having some idea of the time span involved, and it is really not practical to deal with the whole of the past at once: it has to be divided up into manageable slices. But we should always remember that the slices are of our own making: people didn't wake up one morning and say, 'Right, that's the end of the Bronze Age, here comes the Iron Age.' Even if they had, they would still have been the same people, using the same pots and pans with a few new ones, just as we are exactly the same people, in the same houses, on the first day of a new decade or a new government, although in retrospect these might seem to have been important turning points in our own lives or in the history of Britain.

Prehistorians followed this natural habit of dividing up time into slices or periods, and so we have a series of neat segments all ready to use: the Old, Middle and New Stone Ages (or the Palaeolithic, Mesolithic and Neolithic periods); the Bronze and Iron Ages; or even subdivisions – Iron Ages A, B, and C. They also took from historians the practice of naming periods and areas after peoples – or vice-versa – but because there are by definition no written records of the names of prehistory, they had to invent names for the nameless peoples who had made the weapons and pots they were studying. Often, it was the pots themselves or other remains that provided the inspiration, and so we have the 'Beaker folk', and the 'corded-ware people', or perhaps the 'battle-axe people', the 'megalith builders' and many more. Other archaeologists used slightly more abstract terms, such as 'culture'. But recently we have stopped personifying ancient pots quite so confidently and even the main chronological divisions used for so long may soon disappear from the literature, although I suspect they will be replaced by others.

The reason for this is that slices of the past can become obstacles to our understanding of it. Each specialist takes his or her period and tries to see how society developed within it. Inevitably there is a tendency to build fences around territories – each period has a beginning, a middle, and an end, or perhaps a formative, classic, and decadent phase. If one tries to study a very long span of time it looks a bit like a series of waves, with each separate specialist period rising, flourishing and declining before giving way to the next. The boundaries between periods can seem very sharp and sudden simply because they are the bits at the edge, which aren't really studied by either specialist. If nothing else, we need to move the fences every so often to prevent the growth of banked-up artificial divisions.

The prehistoric chapters of this book are so broad in their scope that I could not have used very detailed chronological schemes and I have tried to give approximate calendar dates where it seemed necessary. The later chapters, however, do follow a very traditional sequence, but I have tried to show where this view is inadequate. Although the conventional picture of dramatic change accompanied by violent incursions of new people has some truth in it, there was always a substantial element of continuity, both of people and of their ways of life, even through the most sudden and apparently complete disasters.

I think it is very important to look at the past as a continuous process and not as a series of jumps or slices. Just as the landscape has been visibly shaped by man over the centuries, changed sometimes out of all recognition, but still remains the same landscape underneath, so the peoples living in Britain and their ways of life have changed but are still in part grown from roots deep in the past. The people who built Stonehenge were not all wiped out by later peoples any more than Stonehenge has (yet!) been obliterated. Some of us could be descendants of megalith builders as well as of incoming Romans, Saxons, Danes, Huguenots, Asians, Africans, or anyone else you care to name. The societies of the past are the basis of our own society, and, if we are to understand the one, we need to know something about the other. When looking at the countryside we can only understand the bends in the road if we know that they were laid out around the edges of prehistoric fields.

The places and objects I have chosen to illustrate my theme are partly the very well-known ones, which may be familiar already to many people. They are also those which are best-known to myself, or where recent work has produced new ideas. Another person might have made a different selection from the enormous range of possible material, but I hope mine has been broad enough not to be hopelessly biased. The places I describe in the book include most of the places we filmed, with a few more which I know well, or which seemed important in a particular context. The book differs from the scripts in that it has been written by one person, not two, and, of course, in having more words and fewer pictures. In some cases excavation has continued since filming in 1983 and I have tried to take account of finds made in 1984 and 1985.

I am very grateful to all the excavators who allowed us to interrupt their work by filming, or who have shown me round their sites on other occasions, since I know myself how tiresome that can be when there is not much time left to finish the dig. And to all the people whose brains I have picked on one topic or another.

Chapter 1

Hunters and Farmers

The last Ice Age ended about ten thousand years ago, and most of this book is concerned with the period since then. Before that, we cannot really speak of 'Britain'. Over many thousands of years, during the successive ice ages or glacial periods, and the warm interglacials between, ice-sheets advanced and retreated over the northern hemisphere. The sea rose when the ice melted, and fell when it froze again, while the shape of the coastline changed, partly because of the variations in the volume of unfrozen water in the sea, and partly because, in counterbalance, the land sank under the weight of the ice masses and then rose when the pressure was relieved. The geography and climate of what was to become Britain changed many times: mountains were worn down, hills heaped up and river valleys scoured out or silted up. Even major rivers like the Thames were not always there. Sometimes the land was partly under ice, sometimes it was warm enough for tropical species of plants and animals to flourish. At times Britain was just the northwestern corner of the European landmass, while at other times it was cut off.

The coastline is still changing: the Scillies may have been one or two large islands within quite recent centuries instead of the archipelago of small islands they are now; towns in Kent which now lie far inland were once seaports. At Dunwich on the coast of Suffolk, the Roman and medieval town has long since disappeared into the sea. When I worked on an excavation there we found a few traces of timber buildings, and when we surveyed the coastline against the Ordnance Survey map we could see how land had gone even since the map had been drawn. Parts of the coast fall into the sea every year after winter storms. The Thames barrage is just the latest of man's attempts to act Canute and stem the waves. Yet these are still changes of detail. If we had an aerial photograph of Britain taken

Human tooth from Pontnewydd, north Wales. This tooth is around 200,000 to 250,000 years old, but it has unexpected parallels with teeth of much later Neanderthal skeletons.

during the last ten thousand years much of the outline would be recognizable whenever it was taken, whereas earlier versions would not.

It is also during the last ten thousand years that we can begin to see more clearly what human life was like in the past. There have been people in this part of the world for very much longer than that: some teeth from Pontnewydd in Wales may be 200,000 or 250,000 years old and a skull from Swanscombe in Kent may be even older than that. Stone tools from even earlier periods have been found in various places in southeastern England, including some from deposits underneath, and therefore clearly earlier than, the skull from Swanscombe. Small groups of hunters may have visited Britain simply as part of their seasonal wanderings over Europe, arriving overland to stay perhaps only a few weeks or months before moving back south. We should not forget these people: they visited and perhaps stayed more permanently over hundreds of thousands of years, and their lives may have been far more complex and richer than we can now grasp from the stones and bones which are all they have left. After all, how much of our complex material culture would survive centuries of being ground under glaciers? The plastic-bottle culture might not seem very exciting to future archaeologists.

But it is true that we do not know very much about the first inhabitants of these islands. For one thing, it is very difficult to find and excavate the places where they lived, because these have often been buried under many feet of sand and gravel, brought down by glaciers. The bottom of gravel quarries is where the best sites have been found, and many more must remain deep under the present land surface. Even if we had the machinery for digging such deep sites, or could afford it, how would we know where to look? Also, the temporary campsites which we assume these early people lived in might not have left very substantial traces. The precise dating of such very early sites is also still a problem, although new techniques and more information are beginning to help here.

If this book were to be written in proportion to the length of time that man has been living in Europe, then the last ten thousand years would occupy the last page of a very long book. In fact, the closer we come to the present day the more we know and the greater the detail to be recorded, so that most books, like this one, have the reverse proportions and devote far more space to recent centuries or even decades than to distant millennia.

Hengistbury Head, the promontory which juts out from the south coast near Bournemouth, protecting Christchurch harbour, was one of the places where people settled or camped for a while around the time the ice was retreating for what we sometimes fondly seem to think was the last time. Hengistbury is a vivid reminder of the instability of our coast: some of the paths disappeared in the winter of 1984–5 and notices warn of cliff falls and danger both on top of the cliff and down on the beach. Local people fear that the sea will break across the narrow neck of land below the headland and rush into the peaceful lagoon beyond, flooding the marshes and much of the town, including my mother's house. I hope it will not come to that, but more ancient settlements on the cliff top certainly are being destroyed.

Around eleven thousand years ago, when the site was inland from the sea and you could still walk to the Isle of Wight, hunters camped on what was then a south-facing hillside, well away from the coast. Two thousand years later, when they might have been closer to the sea, but still probably didn't need a boat to get to the Isle of Wight, people again lived for a while on the hilltop. The earlier group lived during the period called the Upper Palaeolithic, the late Old Stone Age, whereas the others belonged to the Mesolithic, or Middle Stone Age. But really they had a very similar way of life and the division is a little artificial. Both groups lived by hunting animals, probably reindeer and wild horse, catching fish and collecting plants. They lived in small groups, moving from one place to another as seasonal resources dictated, and they probably did not build very permanent houses. Perhaps just an extended family camped here, though at other times of the year they may have met up with other groups.

There have been several excavations on Hengistbury Head since it was partly ploughed in 1913 and became a 'collector's paradise' because of the number of stone tools that were turned up. In 1983 we filmed Nick Barton, from Oxford, who was excavating part of the cliff edge before the site fell into the sea, as indeed part of it has done since. His main finds, like those of earlier excavators, are stone tools, complete scrapers and blades and also the debris from their manufacture. He had some rather more high-powered technology than had been applied there before, and was using laser beams to plot very precisely in three dimensions the location of every single piece of stone found. He also had a slightly more primitive experimental method of discovering how far fragments might have moved in the soil after they had been dropped: stones were scattered

Excavator at work on the cliff top at Hengistbury Head, Dorset, where an early settlement site is being eroded away.

Flint nodule reassembled from the flakes and tools it had been made into by a Palaeolithic flint-knapper at Hengistbury.

on the ground where diggers would tread on them on their way to empty soil into the spoil tip, and the position of the stones before and after this heavy trampling was carefully plotted.

Excavators of Stone Age sites have begun to work out many sophisticated ways of extracting more information from the apparently unpromising bits of stone which are their main finds. For a long time these have been studied from the point of view of typology, with differently-shaped tools and flakes grouped in sequences to show how they changed over time and how the tools made in one region differed from those made elsewhere. This ordering of the material has been very useful, but the more complicated schemes sometimes appeared a little remote from the ancient people who made and used the tools. At Hengistbury, by measuring exactly where each piece of stone was, and looking to see if any of them actually fitted together, Nick was able to find tools and flakes which had been struck from the same lump of flint. This meant he could show what order they had been made in, and where each had been dropped, almost like looking over the shoulder of a flint knapper as he moved about the site, making one tool, using it, throwing it away and then making another. More than sixty separate pieces, flakes and tools, could be shown to have been struck from one original lump of stone. Doing this kind of work is like working on a lot of three-dimensional jigsaws with all the pieces mixed up and no picture. It sounds even worse than sticking pots together, which I have spent many hours doing: at least with pots there is often a pattern to guide you. A Belgian archaeologist who works on this sort of material has a roomful of tables with flint spread out, worked on in the intervals between doing something else. He has managed to refit flakes to each other even when the core they were struck from has not been found.

Another way of studying stone tools is to examine working edges very closely through high-powered microscopes. The tiny scratches and chips, the 'microwear' as it is called, which can be seen on the edges can show what the tool had been used for. Experiments with replicas have shown that scraping animal hides, cutting up meat or chopping plants will leave different distinctive traces on the edges of the tools used. Nick Barton and Chris Bergman even went so far as to shoot a fallow deer with small flint-tipped arrows, like the ones excavated, to see what traces that would leave. (The animal had already died from natural causes!) So it is becoming possible to get much closer to the people who lived at Hengistbury so long ago, and to see what they were doing there.

Some early sites have produced organic material, as well as stone, usually because they are waterlogged. One of the best-known sites of the Mesolithic period in Britain is Star Carr, in Yorkshire, excavated

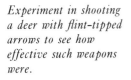

Experiment in shooting a deer with flint-tipped arrows to see how effective such weapons were.

by Grahame Clark between 1949 and 1951. Probably within a few centuries of the second settlement at Hengistbury people lived on, or visited, a site on the edge of a lake at Star Carr, and left a lot of interesting rubbish to be excavated. There were tools and weapons made of bone and antler as well as stone: barbed points, perhaps hunting spears, mattocks for grubbing up roots and pins for fastening skin clothes. There were the bones of the animals which had been caught and eaten, predominantly deer, but also elk,

FAR LEFT *Bone artefacts from Star Carr in Yorkshire, made from the antlers of red deer and the giant elk.*

LEFT *Stag antler frontlet from Star Carr, perhaps worn as a head-dress during religious or ritual ceremonies.*

submerged sites in the shallower parts of the North Sea are probably our best hope of finding out more about this period. One such site has been recently excavated, Tybrind Vig off the coast of Denmark, near Odense on the island of Fyn. Here, under only 10 feet (3 metres) of water, excavators have found the rubbish of a community which lived by fishing and hunting. They have found bone fish-hooks, part of a fishing line, wooden bows and even a decorated wooden paddle, the first sign of artistic ability amongst these people. They were eating seal and porpoise, deer and pig, and also hazelnuts and acorns. There is even a boat, a dug-out log canoe which was used perhaps for eel-fishing, one of the oldest preserved European boats.

For centuries people moved across Britain, northern Germany and Scandinavia, and over the increasingly swampy flat lands now under the North Sea. They hunted game, fished and collected plants in a seasonal round of migration which may sometimes have brought small family groups together in larger gatherings for meetings,

Reconstruction of a Mesolithic settlement, based on information from several excavated sites.

exchange of goods and ideas, and the celebration of a marriage or religious festival. For most of human existence man has lived off the land, exploiting resources as and when they occur. A few peoples still live like this today, although their numbers are visibly dwindling: Eskimos, Australian aborigines and Kalahari bushmen are, or used to be, the best known of such hunters and gatherers, but there are others, though their days seem to be numbered. Once everyone lived like that, and even today in the industrial west many people collect wild blackberries and mushrooms. But from 7000 BC, or even earlier, we can see the beginnings of a new way of life developing in the Near East and around the Mediterranean. Plants and animals were controlled and domesticated, crops were deliberately sown and harvested and animals herded. Farming became the way of life for most of Europe during the succeeding centuries, although it spread fairly slowly in some regions. It had reached Britain sometime before 4000 BC.

Our understanding of exactly how and why this change took place in the Near East, in Britain or anywhere else is still very incomplete. Farming is not the normal human activity it has come to seem: it is an interference with the natural order of things which was a radical departure from the way in which man had adapted to his environment for so many generations. Instead of moving with the herds or seeking out ripe plants at the right season, people had to stay put and take the very considerable risk of investing time and energy in planting crops and feeding animals for delayed and therefore invisible returns. Picking nuts and berries and eating them, or even storing some for later, is a very simple and obvious thing to do. Coming back year after year at the right time to the right place where you know you will find ripe plants needs memory and organization. Hunter-gatherer peoples must have accumulated a vast store of knowledge about such things, perhaps including quite complicated ways of working out what should be looked for when and where. But this is still a long way from the idea of planting seeds, watering and weeding, protecting growing crops against other humans and animals, and then waiting for harvest, all of which involve staying put in one place without the option of moving on if the crop should fail, as the lands around filled up with other settled farmers. It is really less surprising that it took so long for farming to be invented than that it was ever invented at all. There must have been very powerful reasons for giving up old, tried and tested ways of life for something which is in many ways a much harder way of getting food, the time and who need permanent storage, is nonetheless not used only by farmers (and, on the other hand, not all farmers do use it). In Japan pottery was made for a long time before the arrival of farming. Grinding stones can as well be used to grind wild plants as cultivated crops. Domestication will only show after generations of selective breeding, so that the first clear signs in the archaeological record will actually date to a period long after the process began. There is still debate as to whether the people who built the walled city of Jericho soon after 8000 BC were farmers or not.

The differences between farmers and hunters have perhaps also been exaggerated and the change from one to the other seen as more sudden than it was. Interference with nature on a substantial scale may have begun long before full-scale farming arrived. Hunters cull animals of particular ages and sometimes they burn off woodland. Plant collectors may clear unwanted plants so that the ones they want will spread. The recognizable farming practices that are clear in the archaeological record of the Near East from the end of the last glaciation may be the culmination of a very long process, in which people gradually moved from opportunistic exploitation of resources as they found them to controlling and producing them. Claims have been made that land was deliberately cleared in Britain and Ireland during the Mesolithic period, and that indigenous animals such as pigs may have been controlled to some extent long before the conventional package of sheep, goats and cereals arrived.

All the same, sheep and goats are not native to Britain or indeed to northern Europe, and they must have been brought there by someone at some time in the past. The traditional picture is that farming people moved northwards, driven both by the increasing size of their populations and by the exhaustion of the soils they were farming by slash-and-burn methods. Eventually some of the farming communities who had by then been living for some generations in what is now the Netherlands or thereabouts got into their boats, or the boats they had stolen from the Mesolithic fishermen, and crossed to England, to begin an inevitable spread across the whole of the British Isles.

There are scholars who criticize various aspects of this version of events. We don't really know that early farmers did always practise slash-and-burn, or that they didn't learn fairly soon about the advantages of manure, so they need not have been so constantly on the move from land exhaustion. Increase in population may have happened before rather than after the change to farming: it may have

Soay ram from Butser farm, Hampshire, an example of a breed which may preserve many of the characteristics of prehistoric animals.

been the need for more resources to feed a growing population that led to the invention of ways of exploiting the land more intensively through agriculture. The hunters and fishermen of the North Sea region may have been overcome by incoming farming peoples – or they may, after long ignoring such ideas, have eventually been forced into adopting them themselves. Very slight changes in temperature or sea-level might have affected fish stocks, for example. A minimal interpretation of the development of farming in Britain would remove even this apparently firmly founded picture of prehistoric migration.

In place of boat-loads of invading continentals, complete with sheep and sacks of seed corn, this alternative theory would see the native Mesolithic population responding to difficulties which had arisen in part from their own success, producing a population too large to be fed by traditional means, and turning to ideas long current amongst neighbours to the south. Perhaps they went and fetched the sheep and goats across themselves.

The truth is, we do not yet know enough about the size and character of the 'Mesolithic' peoples of the British Isles to say whether they did, or could have, developed into the 'Neolithic' peoples without substantial migration from outside. The fact that it is perfectly possible to argue against what used to look like incontrovertible proof of a migration of farming people from the Continent, even if the argument cannot yet be settled firmly, is a salutary warning against putting too much faith in any of the 'migrations' or 'invasions' of prehistory so confidently described in older literature. We should always look very carefully at our reasons for suggesting it was people from outside who brought about change rather than the local population responding to some crisis by inventing a new way of doing things.

At least it is clear that, once farming had taken hold, it was increasingly difficult for the old ways to persist. You cannot hunt someone else's herds or collect plants from a field you have not sown yourself. Whatever the exact details of the transition, from at least six thousand years ago there are clear signs of the impact of farming in the British Isles – which probably means the process began much earlier.

There seem to have been more people around and they had more material goods. They still had tools made of stone, wood and bone, but they also had pottery. Pottery has been seen as the archaeologist's best friend. Clay can be formed into all sorts of shapes and then decorated in even more different ways. The raw materials, clay and fuel for firing, are fairly widely available, and once the idea has been grasped, pottery is quite easy to make. Once broken, although sherds may be used as lids or scoops, they cannot be recycled in the way that metal objects can be melted down. Pottery lasts well, and doesn't decay in the soil like wood or cloth. So just as the archaeologist studying the Palaeolithic has to reconstruct almost everything from bits of stone, unless lucky enough to find a wet site, so for later periods it is pottery which has attracted the most devoted attention. Different kinds of pots can be plotted to show perhaps (and perhaps not) where different peoples once lived, and the changing styles of pottery over time are still the basis for much prehistoric chronology.

Interpretation is complicated by the fact that pots were used for different purposes. Some pots are burial urns, while others are for cooking or storage. Some people buried their dead in pots, but ate out of wooden bowls or metal cauldrons which have decayed or rusted away. Using potsherds as the basis for our reconstruction of the past is a bit like describing our society using only flower pots or tin cans, while ignoring everything else we use.

Sometimes more than one kind of pottery was in use at one time, and the different types may have had different uses – some for storage, others for religious ceremonies or burial, for example. So the existence of different kinds of pottery is not necessarily evidence for more than one set of people, let alone for assuming that one group had been invaded and overrun by another. Also, although elaborate pots might have belonged initially to the more important members of society, it is often the case that a fashion starts at the top and works its way down. So what might in one generation have been reserved for chiefs and their families might in the next have been copied for everyone. Reassessment of pottery classifications in the light of this kind of rethinking is still in progress, but it looks as if at least some of our 'invasions' may turn out to have been no more than the percolation of a new idea about decorating pots. There might, of course, be very interesting reasons why different patterns came in and out of fashion, but that is another question.

Another way of looking at pots is to try to get some solid evidence of what they were used for. A pot full of cremated ashes has obviously ended up as a burial urn. But it could have been used for something else first, and the potsherds found on settlement sites often don't have any clear context. However, recently developed techniques can help here. Prehistoric pottery was porous, and absorbed substances kept or cooked in it, rather like a modern chicken brick. It is now possible to identify some of the residues still lingering in the fabric of the sherds and sometimes to say if they had been used for cooking porridge or stew. Perhaps we shall eventually have enough information to offer 'prehistoric feasts' as well as 'Elizabethan banquets' as tourist attractions. Again, finding out what pots were used for, like seeing how stone tools were used, gets us closer to the people who made these things, and away from what can sometimes be rather abstract stylistic arrangements in museum cases.

Another aspect of Neolithic life is the manufacture of stone tools on a larger scale than before, with some centres of production perhaps serving far more than their immediate local community. At Langdale, in the Lake District, one source of particularly useful stone was worked extensively, and axes made from this stone have been found far away from their place of origin.

Some kind of exchange or barter system must have been in operation, although it would not have been anything like our modern money economy. At Grimes Graves, near Brandon in Norfolk, there is an open field between serried ranks of forestry pines, where large pits and hollows create a lunar landscape. These are the remains of flint mines, worked thousands of years ago by people who dug shafts through the chalk to get to the seams of precious flint beneath. You can still go down one of the shafts, lit by electricity, by way of a metal ladder, but you have to wear a safety helmet, and metal grilles at the bottom block the side passages to prevent more adventurous visitors from wriggling down them to get stuck or cause a collapse. Like all mines, Grimes Graves must have been an uncomfortable and dangerous place to work, crouched in narrow tunnels with only antler picks and oil lamps, and in danger of sharp cuts from flakes or chips of stone. Although it is now a peaceful and remote place (but for the overhead jet planes), it is as much a piece of industrial archaeology as any other abandoned mine.

As well as the broken pots, bones and stone tools they left lying in the places where they lived or worked, we can see clear signs of how the landscape was changed by the early farmers. In recent years more precise dating methods, and greater application of techniques such as pollen analysis, have allowed a clearer picture to emerge. In particular, the discovery of preserved ancient wood on waterlogged sites has meant that tree-ring dating, dendrochronology, can be linked to dates arrived at through carbon-14 analysis. The tree-ring method works on the principle that trees lay down annual growth rings and that some trees are sensitive to the climate, so that in good years they form a wide ring while in bad it will be thin. Slices through trees showing the pattern of thick and thin rings can be compared and matched to each other, because all the trees of one kind in the same area will react to the climate in the same way, and lay down similar sequences of rings. The overlap between the ring sequences of trees of different ages can be used to produce very long series. For recent periods of the past these sequences begin with the present, with trees which are still living, and so the series can be read back, year by year, to give an absolute calendar date for ancient pieces of wood. In America, where there are trees which live for not just centuries but for thousands of years, the sequence already extends far back into prehistory. In Europe, work in progress is constantly extending the length of the series which we can date precisely.

There are also long series of tree-rings from prehistoric contexts which cannot yet be fixed by relating them to the present, but which can be given approximate dates by using carbon-14 analysis. This works on the principle that all living matter, as long as it is alive, absorbs carbon from the atmosphere, including the isotope of carbon known as carbon-14. Once the matter is dead, the carbon decays – at a known rate. So if the amount still in an archaeological find is measured, it should be possible to work out how long it is since the organism died and ceased to absorb new carbon. There are of course complications both in theory and in practice, but enough samples have now been dated to give prehistorians a framework of dates, independent of the supposed stylistic similarities between objects from different places which used to be an important way of dating, and this framework is constantly being refined.

In the Somerset Levels, flat lands which have in the past been under water, Bryony Orme from Exeter University and John Coles from Cambridge have been working for years on the excavation and recording of ancient wooden trackways found buried in the peat. The peat is now drying out and shrinking from drainage of the land for arable farming, and is also being cut on an industrial scale, both of which activities destroy the pathways of wooden planks or wattle hurdles laid out across the surface of the marsh five or six thousand years ago. When we went to film the Levels we found yet another stretch of trackway in course of excavation in advance of peat cutting. Excavation is very time-consuming as the wood is extremely soft and must be cleaned delicately with plastic spatulae – including those from ice-cream cartons – as metal would damage it too much. Some of the trenches have had diggers suspended above them, lying on their stomachs and dabbling in the mud around the wood, which has to be kept wet as it would shrivel up and crack were it allowed to dry – and would be entirely crushed by boots treading on it!

The earliest track is known as the Sweet Track from its finder, Ray Sweet. It is a plank walkway which rests on a basis of poles, or rails, pegged into the soft ground beneath. The people who built this track about six thousand years ago were skilled woodworkers, and marks of their tools can still be seen on some of the timbers. Later trackways, such as the Walton Heath track, were made from woven

Part of the Abbot's Way, a prehistoric trackway across the Somerset Levels, built around 2500 BC. The surface was made of split alder planks, with branches filling the gaps and pegs driven into the marsh along the sides.

hurdles laid in a long wide path. Some of the tracks have been known locally for a long time, and one is known as the Abbot's Way, reflecting a view that medieval monks and nuns were obsessed with secret passages, tunnels and so on, and so might very well have built mysterious pathways through the marsh. But that suggestion is a few thousand years too late, as both dendrochronology and carbon-14 have clearly shown.

Along the paths a few things were dropped: occasional potsherds, a wooden dish, a mallet made of yew wood, and a long bow, also of wood. It isn't perhaps very surprising that some such things might have been dropped and lost accidentally if someone slipped and fell into the marsh one wet night. So far no bodies of such unfortunates have been found, to match those found in Denmark or even recently in Cheshire ('Pete Marsh' or 'Lindow Man', whose gruesome end is being lovingly chronicled by the British Museum). Perhaps the peat in Somerset isn't conducive to the preservation of bodies, since it is difficult to imagine no one ever did fall in – or get pushed in.

Some of the things that have been found are less ordinary: these include a complete and unused axe made from a foreign stone, jadeite, a beautiful thing which must surely have been valuable to its owner. There is also a wooden figure described politely as 'hermaphrodite'. In later centuries valuables have been deliberately thrown into water as offerings, and perhaps some of the things found by the tracks were also such deliberate offerings.

Perhaps the most interesting aspects of these trackways are less sensational. In the first place, they show that people were organizing themselves to carry out large-scale works, the deliberate connection of one piece of dry land with another for some permanent reason. It is also clear that they were managing the local woodland, planning ahead and growing particular kinds of wood for specific purposes in some considerable quantity. The hurdles were made from woven hazel rods, which means that they were cut from coppiced trees, whose trunks had been cut down to produce new young shoots in the form of a clump of long, thin, narrow wands. Medieval woodland was managed in this way but it seldom is today, except as part of a deliberate conservation policy. The Neolithic communities around the Levels must have been involved in long-term planning and organization on a large scale, in order to grow the right kinds of wood and to lay out the tracks. Dung beetles taken from samples from some of the tracks show that cattle were being driven across them, which implies organization of land for use as pasture as well.

35

Across in the west of Ireland, at Behy and Belderg in County Mayo, there is more evidence of the ability of early farmers to organize on a large scale and of their impact on the landscape. This is another area where peat has been cut extensively for fuel, and years ago a local schoolmaster, Patrick Caulfield, noticed stone walls showing up in the cuttings, under the peat. His son, Seamus Caulfield, became an archaeologist and he now spends his summers investigating this landscape. He has shown that the walls are prehistoric, built before the peat grew up and in some cases over five thousand years old.

The Caulfields took us over the bog, above vertical cliffs going down to sea which that day was calm and blue, though the wind on the cliff almost defeated the microphones. A small rock stack off the coast which has medieval remains on top was another of the sites they had investigated – this involved being dropped from a helicopter onto the very small flat area on top, a drop which had nearly finished Seamus who seemed to have been slightly less enthusiastic about that trip than his father. Fortunately for me, since I have little head for heights myself, I was not called upon to repeat this exploit. The mainland cliffs are now covered in peat, and Seamus showed us how to cut peat by hand, and how the old handcutting of peat had been carried out.

We also climbed into what now looks like a stone-lined hole in the ground, very convenient for one of its more recent uses as an illicit whiskey still. This was originally a tomb built above ground, but the peat has grown up around it and buried it, like the walls. The walls run across the land for miles, in parallel lines back from the sea. They divide the land into long rectangular fields as far as they can be traced under the bog. The walls are quite low drystone constructions which would not have been sufficient to pen sheep, though they might have had hedges or fences on top. But they would have been good enough for cattle, and it seems most likely that is why they were built, evidence that herd management and grassland were the basis for the Irish economy even at that early date. Green fields full of cows are clearly not a new sight in Ireland.

Proof of the date of the field system is given by the remains of a tree which must have begun to grow around the time that the bog was forming, since its roots extended over a thin layer of bog. This tree has been dated by carbon-14, which shows that it began to grow around 3000 BC. The tree grew after the bog had started to form, but the bog must have formed after the walls were built, since it buries them and the bottom courses of the walls rest on the soil beneath. So the walls must have been built before 3000 BC, and perhaps a long time before. There were two trees sitting, as Seamus said, like octopuses on top of a wall, and he was waiting for more dates from these. But it is clear that five thousand years ago or more there were people in the west of Ireland who needed to go to the bother of building miles and miles of stone walls across the country, presumably to keep in their own cattle and to keep out their neighbour's.

These fields were eventually abandoned, engulfed by the peat bog whose clearance is now revealing them again. This peat may have formed because of climatic change – or the farmers themselves may have had something to do with it. It is possible to use pollen samples to show how vegetation and climate have changed in the past, and sometimes it can be argued that it was man who caused the change. Exhaustion of land from overfarming or overexploitation of resources is not a new phenomenon.

Somerset and Belderg are perhaps the most dramatic of recent demonstrations that prehistoric farmers had the ability to clear, control and exploit land on a very large scale from a surprisingly early date. There are many more traces of such activity, some not yet datable, others belonging to a slightly later period than the Irish fields. Dartmoor, like Belderg, may have suffered both from worsening climate and from overexploitation by early farmers. All over the moor there are small stony banks or walls which are locally called reaves. Andrew Fleming, from Sheffield, has studied these walls and he showed me how they run straight across country, even when that means they go down one steep slope and up another – a ruthless division of the land without consideration of topography. They are not easy to see at first, especially amongst the natural heaps and pinnacles of granite, and you need a clear day even when they have been pointed out. The reave we looked at was part of a system enclosing around 7000 acres (2800 hectares), and then beyond that there was another set of aligned fields covering 10,000 acres (4000 hectares) – the modern village of Widecombe sits in the middle of that field system. These fields were laid out around 1700 BC and it is clear that the whole of the area must have been farmed and divided up into very clearly defined territories before 1500 BC.

From excavations of settlement sites that are contemporary with the reaves, the people who built them had a mixed economy, of cattle, sheep, grain and beans. Reaves may have kept cattle out of artificial. To understand one house you really need to excavate the whole settlement and to understand that you need to study the fields, woods and rivers around it, and beyond that, the next village or town and its territory. In the end, there are no limits and the whole of the surface of the earth is one large archaeological site. Perhaps we should study Britain by beginning to dig at John O' Groats and working down to Land's End. Fortunately there are other less time-consuming ways of arriving at some of the answers, aerial photography and field survey being the most widely used, so perhaps some of the questions will be answered more easily. And however interesting their field walls, I think most of us still want to know what people's houses were like, what they ate and drank and in general how they lived.

The best-known early settlements in Britain are not on the mainland but on Orkney, where houses were built of stone, not wood. The earliest so far known is at the Knap of Howar, recently re-excavated by Anna Ritchie. Radiocarbon dates for this site range from 3700 to 2800 BC, yet parts of the walls survive above the door lintel. Finds of pottery, animal bones and fish-bones showed that cattle and sheep were kept and crops grown, but the resources of the sea were also very important – fish, shellfish and sea-birds. This is much the same range of resources as Orkney farmers were exploiting into this century and even now depend on to some extent. A slightly later site on Orkney, at Skara Brae, shows even more vividly what a Neolithic village was like. This village had been covered by a sand-blow until the last century, and it has since been excavated several times, most recently in 1972–3, although much of what can be seen now dates to the work of Gordon Childe in the 1920s. On this windswept island trees do not grow, and so not only the walls but also the furniture were made of stone and have thus survived. The houses are connected by semi-subterranean passages and when houses and passages were all roofed over with turf the whole would have looked more like a giant rabbit warren than a village – some protection against the bitter winter and perhaps quite cosy, if smelly.

In the houses there are the edges of box beds, tanks that were perhaps used for keeping shellfish bait and shelved constructions which are usually called dressers. It is a striking idea to think that five thousand years ago people were already displaying the best pottery where it could be seen as you entered the house – but perhaps that is not a good analogy. These so-called dressers may have been altars, household shrines to the gods – or perhaps simply

Interior of a house at Skara Brae on the Orkneys, showing the stone furniture, box beds, 'dresser', and central hearth. There is a small tank in the floor near the dresser, perhaps for keeping shellfish bait.

convenient places to keep all sorts of things. If you visit Skara Brae in the summer it seems like an idyllic spot, a sandy beach on a peaceful curving bay, the houses quite inviting. In winter you might get a better idea of what life was like for the earliest farmers out here on the edge of Britain, a hard life which meant that few of them lived past thirty and many died in childhood.

Outside Orkney there are very few Neolithic houses and those we do know about now consist only of stone foundations or the marks of wooden posts in the ground. However, we can see that the two basic house-forms which were to recur throughout prehistory, round and rectangular, were already in existence from an early date. A large rectangular house was excavated at Balbridie in Scotland a few years ago. Air photographs and initial excavation had suggested that this was a timber hall of much later date, of the Dark Ages or early

Avebury, Wiltshire.
Part of the stone circle
within the ditch and
bank.

44

stand in the middle of Avebury, or peer through the fence at Stonehenge, most of us also wonder why they were ever built. Why for many centuries, thousands of years ago, was so much effort put into dragging great lumps of stone about the countryside to heap them up into so many different monuments?

Over the years there have been a great many attempts to answer this question. To begin with, prehistoric man – or woman – was not credited with his or her own achievements: the graves were thought to be the homes of fairies, or even more dubious creatures; the stone circles were the petrified remains of girls who danced on the Sabbath, or of kings and their armies; Stonehenge was brought from Ireland by Merlin the magician. More recent explanations call in beings from outer space in flying saucers. Or maybe ancient man himself had supernatural powers, now lost, which enabled him to transport huge lumps of stone by telekinesis and to detect magnetic force fields.

These explanations all seem to me, although interesting as folklore, rather depressing as accounts of prehistory. Why should human effort alone not have been sufficient, without supernatural help? Even serious archaeological explanations have tended to denigrate local people to some extent. The great stone monuments of northern Europe, including Britain, were thought to be copies of ideas worked out first in the Mediterranean – faint echoes of Egyptian pyramids or Maltese temples, the sophisticated models that were copied by northern barbarians. Perhaps there were megalithic missionaries, travelling the seaways of northern Europe to convert the savages living there to whatever religion it was that required the building of large stone monuments. It is of course true that there is a good parallel for this sequence of events – the arrival of Christianity in these islands. This religion, which had and still has profound effects on all aspects of life in Britain, including architecture, was introduced by small groups of foreign missionaries. As I pointed out in Chapter 1, behind many reconstructions of the prehistory of northern Europe lies the consciousness that, in later centuries, so much did come from the Mediterranean. But when radiocarbon dates were calculated for some of the European sites, it soon became clear that this scheme would not work. Some of the northern monuments are very early, built six thousand years ago or more. Even if some of the later ones are contemporary with the pyramids, the idea of building such things cannot have come from Egypt.

Since this realization, thinking about large stone monuments, otherwise known as megaliths, has undergone a profound change. The questions asked now are, firstly, exactly when were they built and how do all the different types relate to each other (for we still have only a bare framework of dates)? Then, how long were they used and how did they change over time? Looking at a tomb or a stone circle like Avebury, and trying to interpret its history as if it is one simple unitary construction, is as much a mistake as trying to understand a medieval cathedral on the assumption that it was built all at once, without allowing for towers collapsing, aisles and side chapels being added or demolished, Victorian renovation and so on. With most of our cathedrals and parish churches we are looking at a thousand years of use. For many of the prehistoric monuments that time could be at least doubled, and their histories may have been every bit as complicated. We would like to know how the megalithic monuments were built, and how they were altered and adapted over time. Above all, we would like to know why they were built, why so much time and energy was channelled into the construction of such things by people who one might have thought had enough to do just staying alive.

Several different lines of thought have been followed by those who have pursued this subject. The most straightforward is the attempt to find out how the stones could have been moved without modern machinery. Medieval cathedrals were also built without the aid of hydraulic cranes, so it is obviously not beyond the powers of ordinary mortal men to do such things. Various explanations, models and calculations have shown how it could have been done, using ropes, wooden rollers and a great deal of brute force. Recently some French archaeologists organized an experiment in which two hundred people heaved a large stone some yards along a field. Enormous stones can be moved without recourse to Merlin or UFOs, so long as one is prepared to expend a lot of patience and muscle power.

There is still debate as to how much mathematics was needed to work out the shapes of the monuments and their alignments. Prehistoric man may have had standard units of measurement and may have known rather more than the basic elements of geometry – or the whole thing may always have been done by trial and error and common sense. There have also been various calculations as to how long it would have taken to construct, say, a large tomb, or Avebury, or Stonehenge. These calculations do not all agree with each other, but they do give a rough order of magnitude in terms of man hours, which can then be combined with calculations of the numbers of men needed to move each stone to give a minimum workforce. For example, if it takes 10,000 man hours to build a long barrow and it needs 10 men to move one stone, then we have 1000 hours per man. If they worked a leisurely 40-hour week that would mean 25 weeks, or 6 months, all at once. But they might of course have worked far longer hours than that, and they might only have worked at building for a few weeks each year. Professor Atkinson once calculated that it would have taken 100 men 3 years and 3 months to build Avebury, and that the larger stones would have needed all 100 to move them.

These figures can only be taken as rough approximations, since they do not allow for a great many possible complications. Above all, we do not know whether there were specialist monument builders, and if so, whether they were privileged beings with plenty of holidays, or slaves worked to death, or whether instead the whole population turned out once a year to work on stone heaving. At least we can say that the building of even a small tomb, let alone one of the large stone circles, shows that people were capable of planning and organization – which is what one might expect from their farming abilities. It also seems that the larger monuments must have drawn on a workforce greater than that which could have been provided by the immediate neighbourhood, so that once such large-scale construction was under way there would have had to have been relationships between communities that begin to suggest larger political or social groupings than the family or clan.

It is a lot less easy to understand why and what for, than how and when. More cautious scholars prefer to concentrate on the last two questions, and say we will never know the answers to the others, though they admit that more digging, preferably on their own favourite kind of tomb, might help. Then there are those who believe that all or some of the stones were set up by astronomer priests whose complex mathematical and astronomical knowledge was not to be matched until the Renaissance, or even till the present century. Others attempt to put the monuments in the context of the society which built them and try to understand what that society was like, how it was organized and how building enormous stone constructions might have fitted in. These two latter approaches are both interesting, and both hold out some hope of getting closer to the megalith builders, but neither is clearly worked out as yet, or without critics.

Professional archaeologists have been very suspicious of astronomical interpretations, equating an interest in the moon with lunacy. One problem is that some of the keenest advocates of ancient astronomy have been mathematicians or astronomers. Their arguments have often seemed to be obscure and all but impenetrable to innumerate archaeologists, who have tended to take refuge in the thought that, if they couldn't understand something, then surely the prehistoric man-in-the-stone-circle couldn't have either. But the body of carefully surveyed and measured sites with apparent alignments on phases of the sun and moon, especially the work carried out by Alexander Thom and his family, have begun to make the subject more respectable, and to dent some sceptics. Clearly there are some deliberate alignments on some very obvious celestial events, such as sunrise or sunset. Midsummer sunrise at Stonehenge is the most famous of these (greeted variously by druids, or by police and barbed wire), if it is visible through the cloud. At Newgrange in Ireland the midwinter sun falls through an opening, the roof box, which must have been built for the purpose, and a ray of light reaches along the passage into the burial chamber, where it could only have been seen by the dead. Something similar happens at Maes Howe in Orkney.

Early man would have been far more conscious of the night sky than we are, without artificial light, and he would have needed a calendar to plan the farming year ahead. There are a number of examples of pre-literate peoples developing calendars, as well as calendrical calculations being amongst the first uses for writing. It would be surprising if prehistoric Britons had not paid some attention to the skies, and had not sometimes taken the sun and moon into account when laying out monuments. But it does still seem very uncertain that they had quite such a detailed and precise knowledge of astronomy as has been claimed. Perhaps we should be slightly sceptical about the existence of wise astronomer priests who designed almost every tomb or standing stone to align with some obscure aspect of the heavens, and who some people have suggested may have lived in the circular enclosures known as henges in great round timber houses or temples, passing on their wisdom through the ages, perhaps to the original prehistoric druids and to who knows whom today. It is even less clear what we should make of recent claims that stone circles produce anomalous ultra-sound readings!

Another approach also uses mathematics, of a rather different kind, in an attempt to discover patterning in the distribution of are related to another kind of burial, so there might be a very specific relationship between the two. Perhaps the dead were seen as in some sense still living in the tombs. If so, it is hardly surprising that later folklore saw megalithic tombs as the homes of other-worldly beings.

It is, however, a bit misleading to use words like 'tomb' or 'grave', since these were not really very like our idea of a burial site: a neat hole containing one body in a coffin with a marker over the top, the place where a single individual has come to an end in physical terms. Neolithic tombs were collective burials, where the remains of many people might be buried. At Waylands Smithy in Oxfordshire parts of more than 40 bodies were found. In the Orkneys, at one large tomb, Isbister, remains of at least 312 skeletons were excavated, while at another, Quanterness, 157 were found during the excavation of part of the tomb, and it was calculated that around 400 may have been put into the whole tomb originally. On the other hand, there are some tombs where hardly any bones, or even none at all, have been found. And the bones are seldom neat complete skeletons. Instead there are piles of bones, sometimes in a heap that all came from one body, sometimes in a pile made up of just one type of bone – all the leg bones together for example, or all the skulls. In some cases it is clear that the bodies had been buried somewhere else for a while before being brought to the tomb, because the bones were not articulated, and some of the smaller bones, or even large parts of the skeleton, were missing. Often it looks as if the grave was subsequently reopened, with bones being added or taken away, pushed to one side or rearranged. This may seem odd or a bit revolting to us, but there are plenty of recorded examples of odd burial practices from the rest of the world which parallel some aspects of what early farmers in Britain seem to have been doing five or six thousand years ago.

The bones do tell us something about the population. There are remains of men, women and children. Most did not live to old age – they would have been lucky to see their thirtieth birthdays and child mortality was enormous. Many had arthritis. All the same, we should be cautious in drawing general conclusions from the bones found in the tombs, as these may very well have been only a part of the population. Even the larger bone collections do not represent a very substantial population if spread over the generations for which some of these places were in use, and in many cases the numbers are clearly too small to have been more than a selected sample. We do not know why they were selected – they may have been the most important members of society, or they could have been sacrifices, or chosen on some completely random basis. At all events, it does not look as if we can extrapolate from the numbers of burials to the size of the population. Prehistoric demography is not an easy subject, and most figures people give are perilously close to having been pulled out of a hat.

Shapes and sizes of tombs vary a great deal from place to place and from one period to another, so that it would be a mistake to offer very general explanations, just as putting all Christian churches and chapels into one category might not be a very helpful thing to do. Some megalithic tombs are very large; there is one at Saumur, in France, which once contained a café, although now it sits rather sadly and damply in the grounds of a new café. At the other extreme, some of the Cornish megaliths, locally known as quoits, are no more than a few large stones propped up against each other, under one roof stone, like a monstrous card house. Some tombs have long

Chun Quoit, the remains of a megalithic tomb, near Morvah in Cornwall.

by small edging stones, with large burnt stones and burnt bones in the middle. (Excavation in 1985 showed that the mound and the platform are only the last phase of a complicated sequence of ritual structures at Crickley.) Again there is the impression that ceremonies outside the tomb (if that is what the mound was) were as important as burials inside it. Perhaps we would incorporate more relevant ideas into our descriptions of these monuments if we called them 'temples' rather than 'tombs'. It is also worth noting that the platform at Crickley was very shallowly buried beneath soil which had never been ploughed. If it had been ploughed, it would have been destroyed, so that it is very possible that other barrows, now apparently isolated in arable fields, once had associated courtyards or platforms.

Some of the most dramatic tombs are those known as passage graves. These have a stone chamber in the middle of a large round mound, reached by a narrow passage. They are found in the Orkneys and in Ireland, in the Boyne valley, although the various people who have tunnelled into Silbury Hill, near Avebury, may have hoped it was a similar kind of burial mound. Their repeated frustration, even when televised by the BBC, may mean that this mound at least never did have anything inside it.

On Orkney Mainland is Maes Howe, a small mound with a narrow stone passage down which visitors can walk, bent double (it is preferable not to use a torch in the impractical if visually effective way I did when we filmed there). There are now no bones or offerings left in the great hollowed stone bowls set in the side compartments of the burial chamber. Perhaps they were taken by the Vikings who left runic graffiti scratched on the walls – most of the inscriptions, like all graffiti, simply say who carved them, but there is also mention of treasure carried away. Even without treasure the place is worth visiting for its masonry alone. The stones are exactly fitted together, and the roof rises to a high beehive shape. It is no wonder that the skill of the masons, as well as the superficial similarity of Maes Howe to some Aegean monuments, like the Treasury of Atreus at Mycenae, led to suggestions of southern influence. But Maes Howe was built long before Mycenae, and any influence would have had to have gone in the opposite direction, though I have yet to hear it suggested that Agamemnon imported masons from the Orkneys.

Newgrange, north of Dublin, is one of Ireland's most famous monuments. It has been excavated and restored so that it now has a wall of white quartz blocks at the front. To some this makes it look like a flying saucer, while others prefer to draw comparisons with public lavatories, but there was evidence for quartz facing on all or some of the mound, if not perhaps in quite such a vertical position as it is now held by official cement. The long tunnel and the chamber at the end are impressive, and at the winter solstice when the sun comes through the roof box this must be a wonderful place to visit. Outside the passage lies a great boulder carved in spiral patterns, a reminder that people had artistic as well as religious sensibilities.

But the passage grave which impressed me most is the one at Knowth, now being excavated by George Eogan, from Dublin. He faces a fearsome archaeological problem, since the tomb is essentially a great heap of stones on top of a central stone chamber,

Interior of the chamber at Knowth, Boyne valley, County Meath, looking up into the roof to show the corbelled structure.

The causewayed camp at Etton, near Peterborough, Cambridgeshire, during excavation by Francis Pryor and Maisie Taylor. In the background the tent covers an area of waterlogged bone and wood in part of the ditch.

At Etton, north of Peterborough, parts of the ditches were still waterlogged, so that Francis Pryor and Maisie Taylor, who are excavating the site, could recover and identify lots of pieces of wood, some of which had been worked. They have also found heaps of bones, 'sheep heaps' as they have christened them, laid neatly along the bottom, and bundles of pork spare ribs, hazelnuts and a whole pot sitting on a birch-bark mat. Even the potsherds found within the enclosure contained food residues, and all these finds support an idea that the camps were places for meetings and feasts, perhaps for fairs like those held in the Middle Ages. The piece of string Francis Pryor has found might have tied up some goods for sale or exchange. Etton could only have been occupied in the summer, because it tends to be under water during the winter. There are other camps which look a bit more sinister: human bones have often turned up, and there were skulls instead of mutton bones in the ditch at Hambledon Hill in Dorset. Were people feasting on their neighbours – or do we have here another part of the burial ritual already glimpsed at the tombs?

Although these causewayed camps do not look as if they were originally defensible, some were later modified. Crickley Hill, and Carn Brea in Cornwall, were both sited on a hilltop position which was perhaps chosen with an eye to defence, and both later had stone and timber ramparts added. Arrow-heads were found at both, and Crickley was partly burnt down. Early farmers are sometimes seen as very peaceful, egalitarian people, but some of them were aggressive enough to put arrows through others who were trying to storm walls built to keep them out.

Later than the causewayed camps are henges. These differ from causewayed camps in that their ditches are usually continuous, broken only at a few regular intervals for entrances. They also sometimes contain circles of timber posts or of stones. Indeed, the name 'henge' comes from the stones of Stonehenge, since Stonehenge may mean something like 'Gallows' or 'Hanging Stones'. The trilithons, the pairs of stones which support lintels to make giant archways, look like early gallows. Stonehenge was for a very long time without those stones, and was initially constructed before 3000 BC as a banked and ditched enclosure around a ring of fifty-six pits, whose purpose is, as they say, 'obscure'. Stones were first added only a thousand years later, first a double circle of

Stonehenge, Wiltshire, a classic view of the monument as it is today.

bluestones perhaps brought from Preseli in Wales, then the massive sarsens we see today. Although the sarsens were brought only from the Marlborough Downs a few miles away, this is still a considerable achievement, considering the size of the stones. Before the stones there may have been earlier timber structures, like the ones found within other excavated henges.

Most of these are banked and ditched enclosures, the banks, as with the causewayed camps, outside the ditches instead of the other way about as one might have expected for practical purposes. Some are very large, like Durrington Walls, not far from Stonehenge, with a maximum diameter of 1598 feet (487 metres), while others, like Stonehenge and Maxey, in the Fens, are smaller, respectively around 320 and 410 feet (97.5 and 125 metres) across. At Durrington Walls and at Mount Pleasant, near Dorchester, concentric circles of holes for timber posts were found, like those already seen from the air at a site near Durrington which was christened 'Woodhenge'. These timber settings have been interpreted as large wooden buildings, suitable homes for the chiefs of a, perhaps, not so egalitarian society, or for the mystic astronomer priests whose arcane knowledge some people think was embodied above all in the most striking of British prehistoric monuments, the stone circles.

Outside the British Isles there are very few stone circles, so that must be one idea we thought of for ourselves. There are over 900 still known, and many more may have been destroyed. They are mostly in the west of England, Wales, Scotland and Ireland, where of course there is the stone to build them. In the east it may be that timber circles remain to be found, like the one which has been photographed from the air at Arminghall, near Norwich.

Stone circles are not all impressive: some have been badly damaged or clumsily restored by well-meaning antiquarians, a fact to be remembered when calculating alignments, since taking a reading from a stone which has only been there for a hundred years or so may not be illuminating about prehistoric astronomy. All sorts of people have dug holes in and around circles, most in search of elusive treasure like golden eggs. Some are hardly visible, like the stones half buried in bracken which I once spent a hot afternoon looking for on Exmoor, in mortal fear of adders. Others sit quietly in pasture, rubbed against by cows, like the Nine Maidens in Cornwall near Land's End. Others have the most spectacular backdrops of scenery, like Stenness and Brodgar on Orkney, near Loch Stenness and the sea. Or Castlerigg in the Lakes, where I sympathized with

PREVIOUS PAGE
Castlerigg in the Lake District, a stone circle set against hills and sky.

the woman who was clearly exasperated by the film crew who had interfered with her peaceful communion with the stones. At least when we visited Stonehenge we went in the cold grey morning before breakfast, the only time archaeologists and film crews are now allowed near the stones, when they will not interfere with anyone except the odd camper in the car park. Perhaps the biggest and the best stone circle is Avebury, where most of the village once lay inside the ring of stones before Keiller bought the estate and began to move the houses out. The main road still goes through the middle.

I do not have an answer to the question of why the circles were built. Perhaps they were used to predict eclipses or to observe the stars and the moon. Or for any kind of ceremony which turns you on – fertility dances involving a fair amount of sex seem to hover at the back of some people's minds. I have heard it said that archaeologists commit both folly and sacrilege by trying to understand standing stones and stone circles through rational argument and excavation, especially by digging trenches with *straight* edges and using *metal* tools. Maybe we should put them back in the context of the other prehistoric monuments we have looked at, and see the circles as a stage in the development of a coherent system, which does have some internal logic, even if we do not understand it.

Stone tombs began with a focus on the bodies of the dead buried inside them, but they seem to have increasingly developed as places where ceremonies in the forecourt outside took on more significance. On the other hand, human bones were sometimes buried in or near the later monuments, henges and stone circles, and some of these are associated with groups of stones called 'coves' by antiquarians, which could be seen as vestigial stone tombs. At Crickley the platform in front of the barrow was circular, edged with small stones. It may be that stone circles were simply the next stage in the development of the courtyard areas of tombs, and took over the functions of these places, perhaps an indication that the burial aspect of religion was becoming less important. All these monuments, tombs and circles, and perhaps the causewayed camps and henges as well, could be seen as part of one long evolving tradition, from before 4000 BC when the first tombs were built, to around 1100 BC, when it was still worthwhile for people to extend the avenue of stones which leads to, or from, Stonehenge.

Rows of stones form another part of the picture, and they too may have developed from earlier monuments, long, narrow, banked and ditched constructions known as cursuses. This name comes from an

idea that they might have been ancient race-tracks – as good an explanation as any other that has been put forward for these odd features, which run for miles across country. One north of Stonehenge is 2 miles (3 kilometres) long and another runs across Dorset for $6\frac{1}{2}$ miles ($10\frac{1}{2}$ kilometres). In the east of England one near Maxey disappears into the fen, so its full length is unknown. As well as race-tracks, cursuses have been seen as ceremonial or processional ways, or as yet more places for leaving bodies out to decay. Any or all of these functions might have been taken over by the stone rows – or both kinds of monument might have had other and as yet unthought of purposes. Some stone rows are paired to form avenues, as at Stonehenge or at Callanish in the Hebrides. At Merrivale on Dartmoor, stones run across the moor with no very clear end or beginning, near the remains of prehistoric huts. None of the English stone rows compares with the Breton site of Carnac, where row upon row of stones runs through the gorse.

Single stones, or stones in groups of two or three, are also strewn across the country. Three in a row can be seen from the A1 near Boroughbridge in Yorkshire, the Devil's Arrows. Again, none of the British stones is anywhere near the size of one Breton stone, 'Le

Stone row on Dartmoor, at Merrivale.

Grand Menhir Brisè', which lies in pieces on the ground. I remember several learned professors attributing its original erection to the effects of magic potion, maybe an early version of Calvados.

One of the interesting things about all the monuments I have been describing is the way in which they often occur near to each other. In some places there is what one might call a ritual landscape, where for thousands of years people used and modified the same monuments, as well as building new ones nearby. The best known of these lies around Stonehenge, and has recently been remapped in great detail by the Royal Commission on Historical Monuments. Here in the space of a few square miles there are the henges, Stonehenge, Durrington Walls and Woodhenge, two cursuses, and a multitude of barrows, including both the earlier long barrows and later smaller round ones. The same thing can be found elsewhere, where again a whole landscape is covered with monuments. At Kilmartin in Argyll there are seven stone cairns over burial chambers, set in a row along the valley. Nearby is a stone circle, and also rocks marked with hollowed-out 'cup-and-ring' marks. Over in the east of England air photographs and field survey have shown how complex prehistoric features have been buried by silt or peat, but are now reappearing as the land shrinks from drainage. Near Maxey, not far from Peterborough, there were henges, a cursus, and many other kinds of prehistoric enclosures. In other parts of the country similar complexes may have long since disappeared under cities or roads, or simply have been ploughed out.

There are also many instances of the building of one monument on top of another, like the passage grave at Bryn Celli Ddu in Wales, which was put on top of a henge (though someone has recently suggested that the two are contemporary, so that this is really one monument and not two). Another example is the chambered tomb within the stone circle at Callanish. There are also much later examples, where Christian churches have been built on top of earlier monuments, like the ruined Norman church at Knowlton in Dorset which sits within a henge.

The important thing is that there does seem to have been, to some extent, both continuity of use and in attitudes to ritual and its place in society and the landscape, which lasted for thousands of years. Of course religious belief can be passed on to new peoples, and incomers can venerate the shrines of the natives they have defeated. But one might also argue that the sequence as a whole suggests stronger elements of continuity. The same ritual places were clearly hallowed for centuries, and some aspects of the treatment of the dead may have remained the same. This could well mean that there was a continuing element in the population, whatever new groups may have been absorbed from time to time, whether peacefully or otherwise.

Even when new kinds of monument develop they may have more to do with changes in society than with invaders from outside. The transition between the Neolithic and Bronze Ages used to be seen as a very dramatic break, brought about largely by the agency of invaders with a new kind of pottery, a new burial rite, and the knowledge of metal. These were the Beaker folk, called after their pottery, who buried their dead under small mounds, now called round barrows. This was an individual burial rite for specific people, contrasting with the earlier mass interment of bones of the ancestors in the old

Handled beaker from Fordham, Cambridgeshire, with elaborate incised decoration.

long barrows. The beakers were so-called because to their first discoverers they looked like beer mugs – some of them do have handles and do indeed look like tankards, but far more are handle-less jars with a variety of incised decoration. This type of pottery has been found all over Europe in burials which also contain distinctive artefacts, such as delicate stone arrow-heads and wrist guards of stone made for archers, and sometimes metal objects as well. The people have been thought to belong to a new skeletal type, with differently shaped skulls from the native population. They are still secure in many books as an invading warrior élite, who quickly established themselves as rulers over the subjugated natives. Yet every detail of this picture has been challenged and Beaker folk have descended from warrior aristocracy, to missionary priests, to purveyors of magic potions in their beakers – or simply to a 'cult with alcoholic overtones' taken up by the native élite. So we may be left, not with an invasion, but with the invention of alcohol, in itself of course a revolution if people really had not known its delights before!

This shift in interpretation is partly a reflection of an antipathy to the recognition of any invasions at all in prehistory, but it is also true that the last picture fits the facts as well as the first and is at least as likely. Even the apparently firm skeletal evidence is not secure, since we do not have enough complete Neolithic skeletons from the areas and periods where beakers first appear to see if there really is a dramatic and sudden change in physical type. This whole subject is in need of more modern anthropological investigation. Again, the use of single mounds for single burials was not unknown in the earlier period: not everyone was buried in a mass grave in a long barrow, or left lying about in the ditches of henges and causewayed camps. It could very well be that the habit of being buried with large decorated pots, which may have contained alcohol, together with the knowledge of metal, was something which spread as a fashion to Britain, to be taken up by local leaders first, filtering down only gradually to the rest of the population.

Another 'invasion' which used to be attributed to the early Bronze Age is that of the Wessex chieftains, warriors again, but this time from Brittany. There are strong similarities between the bronze weapons found in Brittany and those found in southern Britain, and there must indeed have been contact between the two areas, but it need not have been violent. This 'Wessex culture' is partly defined by gold jewellery, much of which may have been made by one skilled craftsman: the genius of an individual goldworker, and trade

View along the ramparts at Maiden Castle, Dorset.

defence against ravaging hordes of invaders – or neighbours – seems to have been the paramount concern. It is perhaps not surprising that until recently invasion has played a large part in the interpretation of this particular slice of prehistory. After all, it ends with a very well-known invasion, that of the Roman army, and before that we have Caesar's account of the Belgae crossing from Gaul to Britain. And there is always the question of the Celts. Some people have tried to identify Celtic or Belgic invasions in the archaeological record, while others have contented themselves with non-committal labels like Iron Age 1, 2, and 3, or else they have invented new names. The Marnians, for example, were thought to have come from the Marne region of modern Belgium, while the Arras culture of Yorkshire takes its name from a local site, and not, as one might have thought, from the continental Arras.

One can hardly deny the Roman conquest, although I hope to show in the next chapter how some aspects of it were less complete than one might think, and I would not like to call Caesar a liar, so some Belgae had better stay, though whether their name should be attached to so many pots and sites as it has been is open to question. But some of the other 'invasions' look less secure. The Arras culture, for example, involves an elaborate burial ritual in which some people, probably chiefs and their families, were buried in chariots or carts. Several more such burials have been excavated recently at Wetwang Slack in Yorkshire. Very few other burials of any kind are known from Iron Age Britain – it was one of those times which are most exasperating for archaeologists, when dead bodies were disposed of in some way which leaves no traces. Maybe people were cremated and their ashes scattered to the winds or sprinkled in a river, like modern Hindus in the Ganges. Or maybe they were left out for animals to eat – or simply buried without any diagnostic grave-goods, like medieval and modern burials. Chariot or cart burials are not known from other parts of Britain, but are fairly widespread on the Continent, and again the simplest way to account for the spread of the idea might seem to be yet again to conjure up

An Iron Age burial at Wetwang Slack, Yorkshire, excavated by J.S. Dent in 1984. The wheels belonged to a chariot or cart which had been dismantled before burial. With the skeleton were a sword, spearheads and horse trappings.

A bronze crater, or wine-mixing vessel, found in a burial at Vix in eastern France. It is 5 feet (1.64 metres) high and was probably transported in pieces from somewhere in the Mediterranean world to be reassembled in France.

who were perhaps continuing a tradition of forceful aristocracy first witnessed in the Iron Age.

Around the Heuneberg are burial mounds, including one very large one, the Hohmichele. This contained several burials, most robbed long ago but still with some traces of the wealth originally deposited, such as a wagon, bronze harness equipment, and silk threads. The fort itself was built on a spur of land overlooking the Danube valley and was probably sited to control trade passing along that valley. Part of the interior has been excavated and shown to have been densely occupied, with rectangular timber buildings set out in rows and rebuilt many times. The finds include many imports from the Mediterranean such as fine pottery and Etruscan bronze jugs, and also local copies of such things. Even the ramparts showed signs of foreign ideas: one phase was constructed in mud brick, not a building material normally used in damp European climates, though these walls did survive for some time. There were also projecting towers, another feature alien to European hillforts. Mud bricks and towers are Mediterranean ideas: the rulers of the Heuneberg were clearly importing builders and their expertise as well as bronzes and pottery. Greek traders and craftsmen may have visited or even lived there permanently, but there is no historical suggestion of a Greek or Etruscan campaign up the Danube, and no reason to suppose that any other than native rulers lived and were buried there.

The Heuneberg is not the only place where barbarian chiefs were enjoying Mediterranean luxury. In eastern France, at Mont Lassois, is another fort also sited close to burial mounds. One of these mounds, at Vix, contained amongst other things a monstrous bronze vessel, as tall as a man, a crater or wine-mixing jar. It looks as if this had been transported in sections and reassembled at the other end, as there are Greek letters scratched on it which look like the equivalent of 'slot A', or 'side B'. Given the size of the jar, this would not be at all surprising. If, as classical authors claimed, barbarians were willing to give a slave for only one amphora of wine, one wonders what was given for enough wine to keep the Vix crater full!

The effect of Mediterranean civilization to the south may have been more far-reaching than just leading to the exchange of goods. The existence of wealth like that shown at the Heuneberg and at Vix, and the inequality in society which it must reflect, may have arisen partly from that trade. If prestige and power depended on the display of extravagance, whether by heaping up goods for oneself or by giving them away to followers and dependents, then access to with 6 miles (10 kilometres) of ramparts, some still standing as high as 15 feet (4½ metres), enclosing over 750 acres (300 hectares) of land. Again, the defensive aspect was important and sections were cut through the banks and ditches which form a complex sprawling series of enclosures over an area now occupied by several large fields and scattered houses. Part of one of the Wheelerian trenches is still open, and standing in the bottom of the rock-cut ditch it is easy to relate to the dramatic story Wheeler was able to weave from historical sources and his own excavations. Queen Cartimandua of the Brigantes quarrelled with her husband, Venutius, some time during the AD 50s and ran off with his armour-bearer. Eventually she appealed to the Romans for assistance against her husband and they seized the opportunity to expand north. Stanwick could have been the site of Venutius' last stand in AD 74 against the Roman general, Cerealis. Parts of the defences were unfinished, and showed signs of hasty modifications in the face of imminent attack.

This is a memorable story and it did seem to fit the evidence, and also to support the view that hillforts were primarily elements of military strategy, thrown up sometimes in haste to meet short-term threats, essentially defended enclosures and places of refuge. Yet Wheeler's own excavations at Stanwick and at Maiden Castle did involve investigation of parts of the interior, which began to show that these places had been rather more densely occupied on a more permanent basis than he himself had suggested. Simply looking at Stanwick one wonders about its defensive nature. For a start it is not on top of a hill, and it is an enormous rambling complex. Not all of it could possibly ever have been seriously defended, as Wheeler himself said. Recently the Royal Commission on Historical Monuments has resurveyed the site and it has also been further investigated by Percival Turnbull, who excavated a small area in the interior. Before this excavation, a much larger part of the site was covered by a magnetometer survey, which picked up the outline of disturbances under the surface, probably pits and ditches.

The picture emerging from this work is of a site occupied some years before the famous quarrel of the Brigantian rulers, and its origins are seen not so much in terms of a military response to invading forces as of an economic response to the new trading opportunities opened up by the presence of the Roman army in the southern half of Britain. Stanwick lies near the junction of two routes, south to north along what is now the A1, once the Great North Road, and east to west across the Pennines, so it could have been a sort of prehistoric Scotch Corner. It may have been the place where the wealth of the local region was tapped by its rulers through fairs or markets under their control, and where goods were traded with merchants from the south. In the early phases it may not have been strongly defended, and it is not even clear that the later defences were deliberately slighted at the time of Cerealis' attack.

Stanwick is an enormous site and more work is needed there before it can be fully understood, but it does now look as if it had more importance as a local centre, and for a longer time, than as a bulwark against Roman attack. Another hillfort, Danebury in

Skeletons in the bottom of a pit at Danebury in Hampshire, excavated by Barry Cunliffe.

In Ireland stone-walled forts are called cashels. In County Clare there is one at Cahercommaun, which sits on top of a steep cliff, and another at Ballykinvarga which is surrounded by sharp stones in serried ranks, which would have broken any cavalry charge and made even attack on foot more difficult.

Then there are the underground passages or chambers, the souterrains – or fogous as they are called in Cornwall. We found one in an Irish rath which led from the middle of the enclosure under the bank to emerge in the side of the ditch. A spy could have squeezed in or out here during a siege, but an enemy could equally well have got in. The first time I went there with students we all squeezed through, from the rabbit-hole-like entrance in the ditch through the small passages and rooms underground, where we had to crawl or wriggle on our stomachs, past the remains of incautious sheep who had fallen or wandered in and never climbed out, to emerge in the very small stone-lined opening in the middle. All of us, even the

Entrance to an underground passage or fogou at Boleigh, Cornwall.

largest, did successfully squeeze through and I don't suppose many Iron Age people were larger than modern students, so they certainly could have used it as an uncomfortable way in or out.

Experiments by intrepid Irish students showed that the temperature below ground was no lower, and might have been higher, than the temperature in a caravan above ground, so perhaps the souterrain was for sleeping in. Another possibility is that they were used for storage, and would probably have been no more inconvenient than a modern attic. I fear when we filmed there we did not get the cameras underground, as it seemed hazardous enough to film at the entrance where a still-living but dubiously friendly sheep was in possession.

Several surviving prehistoric settlements in Cornwall have the remains of fogous, usually fairly short stone-lined passages which would have been suicidal as refuges since anyone inside could easily have been smoked out or burnt to death. Some people have suggested fogous were actually shrines, perhaps to an earth goddess, suitably dug into the earth. The owner of one fine example, who let us troop through his garden to look at it, suggested we should try to think ourselves back into the minds of prehistoric man in order to understand fogous, and he may well be right – if one could but do it. So it may be that fogous are connected with ritual rather than with defence, or perhaps they are just complicated larders.

In Scotland there are a great many different kinds of defended site. There are the romantic-sounding vitrified forts, where the timbers within stone and earthen banks have been fired, creating so much heat that the stones have become glassy and fused together. There are smaller, stone-walled forts or duns, and there are the stone towers known as brochs. These are round, with thick walls pierced by narrow chambers and stairways, and a central living area which was once of more than one storey. Around many brochs are the remains of other smaller buildings. These used to be dismissed as later accretions, but should perhaps be seen as part of the original complex, with the tower as refuge in time of trouble. Most brochs only survive a few feet above ground now, but the one we filmed at Gurness on Orkney still gives some idea of what the interior once looked like. It used to be thought that brochs were a comparatively late and short-lived phenomenon, perhaps something to do with response to Roman pressure or influence from further south, but some have now been shown to have been built many centuries before any Romans set foot on English soil, let alone penetrated Scotland, million timbers to construct a platform that large. This is an awful lot of trees and most of them cannot have been growing very close by, especially not the oaks. Whoever built the platform had a very powerful incentive to get away from it all, as he or she could perfectly well have lived on dry land half a mile away at Fengate.

This site seems likely to be one of the most interesting of recent prehistoric excavations, since the preservation of the timbers by waterlogging means that much detail can still be seen. The points of the posts rammed into the platform have axe marks as clear as when they were cut. And the lower half of a very large building still survives. It was rectangular, about 23 feet (7 metres) wide and much longer, with walls consisting of upright posts with panels of bark between, and rows of internal aisle posts. There is a doorway with a wooden threshold still in position, and a plank floor dusted with fine white sand. If the diggers manage to prevent themselves from falling into the noxious waters of the dyke, while keeping the wood wet to stop it shrivelling up and disintegrating, Flag Fen should give us the best view we have had of a prehistoric house since Skara Brae emerged from the sand.

The fact that the house is rectangular is interesting, as on the whole most excavated prehistoric houses in Britain seem to have been round. But there were large rectangular houses on the Continent and, if there is anything in the idea that stone tombs were 'houses for the dead', their often rectangular plan might well have been reflected in houses for the living. One Neolithic rectangular timber building at Balbridie in Scotland has already been mentioned, excavated in the belief that it was a Dark Age hall, by analogy with other sites where early medieval or Anglo-Saxon timber halls have been found. Perhaps we should be more cautious in identifying the plans of buildings seen on air photographs as being Anglo-Saxon palaces or halls, in case they are also much earlier. One of the limitations of air photography is that although you can identify some features with near certainty, such as Roman forts or Saxon burials, you can only be sure of your interpretation if the site is excavated.

Flag Fen is also interesting because it is a defended site of a fairly early date, the later Bronze Age. 'Iron Age forts' used to be assigned to the last few centuries before the advent of the Romans, whereas it now looks as if some were much earlier. For the best part of a thousand years the nature of society was such that people felt that it was worth devoting much of their energy to defence, or a display of defence. Of course, the next two thousand years have not really been so very different, in that we have gone on devoting much of our energies and resources to war. From Iron Age forts and Roman camps or medieval castles we have progressed to gun emplacements, army camps and tank training grounds, all of which have left their mark on the landscape.

It is also important to find evidence for such a defended site in the east of England. The lack of hillforts in East Anglia is fairly readily explained by the lack of hills, and stone forts in upland stony grazing lands are clearly much more likely to survive than earth and timber forts in arable country. Even so, there are still a few fortified sites in the east. There is a well-preserved fort at Warham camp in Norfolk, one of the few parts of the county where ancient grassland remains. There is another in marshy land near the coast at Holkham, somewhat fly-infested, but a useful ostensible goal for expeditions in reality dedicated to swimming in the sea and consuming fish and chips in Wells, followed by beer in Nelson's birthplace.

What were all these forts for? Clearly, they were partly designed to keep out the neighbours. Rising population and a worsening climate may have combined to produce land hunger as areas like the west of Ireland and then Dartmoor and other uplands had to be abandoned. Or society may have begun to set a premium on military prowess, with status measured by success in war. Accounts by classical authors, and also later Irish literature, can be used with a great deal of caution to reconstruct a picture of Iron Age society as one where men were always ready for a good fight. They might fall out over dinner, or run off with each other's wives, daughters or cattle. If cattle were the principal form of wealth, the quickest way to get rich would have been to drive off someone else's cattle herd, although that would of course invite the inevitable retaliation. Foreigners in one guise or another may have caused complications from time to time, including armed invasions, but it does look as if the natives were perfectly capable of causing enough trouble for each other to be in need of their forts and fennogs to sleep safely at night. And invasions cannot have been happening continuously for nine or ten centuries.

Inequality and strife may also have been fuelled by metal, first bronze and then iron. Stone axes have usually been seen as peaceful tools for cutting down trees, and even arrow-heads as mostly associated with hunting. But swords are not ploughshares, and when we see bronze and then iron swords of increasing length and sharpness appearing, our thoughts turn to battle. However, this contrast should not be overemphasized. At Crickley Hill, stone arrow-heads ended up in the backs of people, not animals, and an axe would make a good blunt weapon for bashing someone over the head. Nor should we exaggerate the initial impact of metal. Many people went on using stone tools long after the first bronze axe had been cast in Britain, and likewise bronze was still used after the start of iron production.

It used to be thought that the discovery of iron was a secret first worked out and then closely guarded by the Hittites, and that only after their empire's collapse around 1000 BC did the ability to make iron tools and weapons spread around the Mediterranean, reaching north into Europe in the following centuries and automatically superseding bronze wherever it appeared. In fact, knowledge of iron may have been around for a very long time, despite the fact that it is more complicated to manufacture than other metals, but it may not have seemed very attractive. Until smiths developed fairly sophisticated methods of working iron, objects made from it were brittle and actually less useful than good quality bronze. It may have been that demand for bronze increased to the extent where it overtook supply, with some sources of copper or tin perhaps worked out or inaccessible because of war. At this point, the more plentiful iron ores could have been turned to as a second best. Of course, once the difficulties of processing it have been mastered, iron is better than bronze for sharp tools and weapons, and those who possessed good iron swords and spears would have had considerable advantages over anyone still using bronze rapiers.

Bronze is, however, more decorative than iron, and it may be that it was not just sharp blades but also the elaboration of the decoration associated with them which mattered. Wealth and therefore power might have been demonstrated by the flashiness of men's swords, shields and helmets, belts and brooches, as also by the harnesses of their horses and chariots, or the gold necklaces of their women and the bronze vessels on their tables. Although there are few burials in Britain, apart from the chariot burials in Yorkshire, to demonstrate such a love of display, there are wealthy cemeteries on the Continent which do. Many of the objects found are decorated in styles which have been called after two places, Hallstatt and La Tène.

Hallstatt is today a picture-postcard village in Austria, with wooden houses built out over a lake beneath classic mountain scenery. There are salt-mines in the mountains which were the basis for the prosperity and fame of the region around 700 to 400 BC. The mines are reached today by a funicular railway, and it is possible to go inside them. But cameras do not like a salt-laden atmosphere, so we didn't go in, but contented ourselves with filming some miners marching stolidly out. On the lower slopes is a cemetery, many of the graves from which were excavated in the nineteenth century but fortunately quite well recorded. Some contained bronze or iron swords, axes and helmets, also bronze vessels and jewellery, a few of which are exhibited in the village museum. But I have to admit that the most memorable exhibit in Hallstatt is an assemblage of the skulls of fairly recent inhabitants, with their names painted upon their bony foreheads.

By 400 BC another site, the Dürrnberg bei Hallein near Salzburg, also a salt-mine, had taken over the position of Hallstatt in this part of Austria. Rich finds from the cemetery here are displayed in the museum at Hallein. There we filmed some of the bronze vessels, jewellery and reconstructed burials, with myself peering rather unnecessarily into the glass, speechless because we did not have the sound man with us.

More familiar to British eyes is the art style named after the Swiss site, La Tène. The later versions of this style became popular in Britain in the last centuries before the Roman conquest, and then it surprisingly re-emerged centuries later as 'Early Christian' art and has been around ever since under various 'Celtic Art' guises. This art style involved abstract rather than naturalistic designs, flowing curvilinear motifs in a balanced dynamism rather than perfect symmetry. There is perhaps a suggestion of plant tendrils, and stylized heads of animals or humans may appear. The designs can be raised, as repoussè, or engraved or cast with coloured inlays. Red coral, red glass and red enamel occur most often in the designs, but other colours, such as yellow, were also used. It is the metal objects that have survived, mostly bronze, but there may have been textiles and wooden carvings as well: from the later Viking period we have just enough of such perishable objects with elaborate ornament to show how much has been lost. How peripheral some of the smaller metal dress-fasteners might have seemed to the people who used them, whereas now they are the cornerstones of complicated classification schemes! Even human flesh may have been decorated – the famous ancient British woad may have been tattooing, like the tattooing preserved on the skin of a deep-frozen Scythian from Russia.

Many of the best-known pieces are now in the British Museum. There is the Battersea shield, still lovely however many times one sees it illustrated or reproduced in replicas, also bronze helmets and a fair number of sword scabbards. There are heavy bronze arm-rings with red and yellow settings and brooches like large safety pins, in bronze or silver. The bronze mirrors may not have given a very clear picture of their owner in their polished surfaces, but the backs had delicate intricate patterns. More functional objects were also decorated, like the metal parts of horse or chariot harness and even iron firedogs, with elegant stylized animal heads at each corner.

Above all, when one thinks of metal of this period it is gold which comes to mind: great gold torcs, neck rings made from tubes of gold or twisted wires, with looped terminals decorated in curving patterns. Many have turned up in East Anglia, recently as well as in

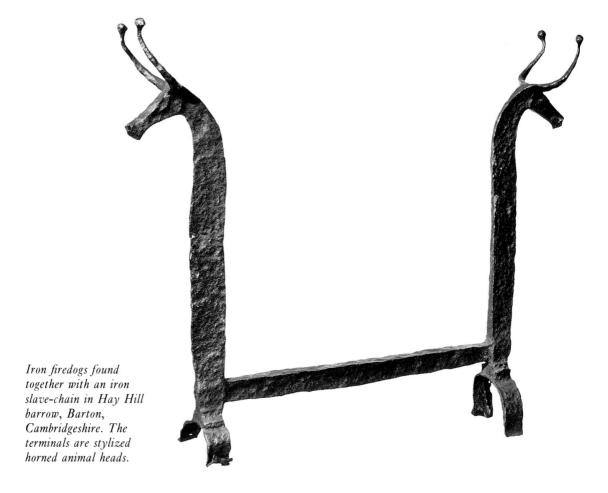

Iron firedogs found together with an iron slave-chain in Hay Hill barrow, Barton, Cambridgeshire. The terminals are stylized horned animal heads.

96

Bronze mirror with La Tène pattern on the back, found near Great Chesterford, Essex.

the past, sometimes amazingly dismissed as bits of old brass bedstead on first sight. East Anglia was the home of Queen Boudica (Boudicca to the not quite so modern and Boadicea to the even older!), and there is a description of her wearing a great gold necklace which was perhaps one of these torcs. Celtic chiefs and warriors must have been a colourful lot dressed up for a feast or a battle, and colourful in other ways, trying to prove by the lavishness of their hospitality, the size of their ramparts or the weight of gold around their own or their wives' necks, that they were more important than their rivals. As usual, this exciting if at times precarious existence of the upper classes was sustained by the solid mass of the people. Their lives were perhaps less exciting, but it was their efforts which produced the wealth in grain, cattle and minerals, as well as the manpower to build the forts.

Although the homes of these more ordinary people have not left such dramatic remains as the aristocratic hillforts, we do know quite a lot about their lives. There are even several places where we can still see parts of an Iron Age village, and get some idea of what it would have been like to live there. In Cornwall there are stone-built houses whose walls still stand (with a bit of reconstruction) at Carn Euny and at Chysauster. There are courtyard houses at both places, conquest. We know about these people and others mostly because they were the rulers the Romans came into contact with, and either defeated, or maintained as client rulers for a time. We also know about them from their coins, which seem to copy an idea they must have learned from contacts with the Continent.

The centres of these tribal kingdoms were not always in inaccessible hillforts, but rather they were large enclosed areas known to scholars now as oppida, the Latin word for towns. It isn't clear whether oppida were densely occupied, like a Roman or medieval town, or whether they were simply places where the chief lived and kept his cattle herds, and summoned his army and the rest of the population for war or feasts. A recent survey of Camulodunum, for example, does not seem to show that the very large area occupied by the Iron Age oppidum was full of buildings or even storage pits. These places are rather like Stanwick – indeed, Stanwick appears on lists of oppida as well as those of hillforts, which shows how imprecise the distinction is. Perhaps the economic, social and political functions of forts and oppida were very similar, with the diminished emphasis on defence at oppida reflecting either new methods of warfare, or better order imposed by stronger kings.

It is interesting to speculate on what would have happened if Claudius had failed in AD 43 as Julius Caesar had failed in 55 BC. What would Britain have looked like if there had been no Roman conquest? Part of the answer can be suggested by looking at Ireland, which was not conquered, but even before AD 43 there were differences between Britain and Ireland which might make that parallel difficult to pursue, at least for southeastern England. The tribal divisions which existed during the last decades before the Roman conquest, and the way in which some units grew at the expense of others and then collapsed, suggest a situation very like that which was to reappear after the end of Roman rule. Then there were petty kingdoms again for centuries, of Anglo-Saxons and Britons, which were only gradually welded into the larger units of England, Scotland and Wales. In the long term, one could almost see the Roman conquest as a hiccup in the development of Britain. But it certainly did not look like that at the time, nor has it seemed that way to most people who have studied it.

Chapter 4

Romans and Countrymen

The Roman Empire is something most of us think we know all about, and we can relate to life in Roman Britain far more easily than to prehistoric society. The Romans, like us, had roads, drains, a water supply and even public baths. They washed, cleaned their fingernails and shaved their beards. They had comfortable houses with underfloor heating, and massive public buildings adorned with marble statues of the great and the good. They had schools, doctors, theatres and sport – though even modern football falls short of the savagery of some ancient sports. They suffered from some of the same social and economic problems as ourselves: there was great inequality with the rich living in ostentatious luxury and sometimes enjoying scandalous lives, alongside the masses of rural peasantry and urban poor. In Rome there were even jerry-built flats and state hand-outs. There was corruption in high places and heavy taxation to pay for a large army and an even larger bureaucracy. It all seems horribly familiar.

We know so much about them because, when not building flats in Rome, they built to last. All around the Mediterranean and in western Europe 'Roman remains' still litter the ground, ranging from stubs of walls to a complete amphitheatre or wall circuit. Even in Britain, after centuries of stone-robbing and decay, there are still substantial chunks of masonry standing above ground, and quantities which have been dug up from beneath. We also have enough of the pottery, jewellery and other detritus of Roman life to furnish these ruins, so that we can create interiors like the one at the Museum of London which gives an illusion of looking at a Roman house. However, perhaps we should remember that we are not really looking at a Roman house, and that such reconstructions usually embody far more of the period style of those making them than is from epic films of dubious authenticity or from television, but at least some sort of an outline lingers. Most of us have a smattering of classical mythology, often in a rather Victorian version, but enough to give us some clue as to the meaning of odd references to Venus or Hercules.

A great deal is known about the Roman Empire and life in it. Contemporary literature includes not only poetry and plays but also histories, biographies and, of course, mountains of legal and administrative documents. There are also letters, some of them written by quite ordinary people. In Egypt papyri with all manner of litigation and private letters on them have survived because of the dry climate: at the other end of the Empire, in Britain, it is instead the damp which has preserved messages written on wood. One such letter, sent to a soldier serving at Vindolanda on Hadrian's Wall, mentions sandals, socks and warm underpants, perhaps sent by a mother to her son freezing on the frontier. Less agreeable but equally vivid insights are offered by the lead curses found at temples or shrines, in which deities are asked to wreak vengeance on those guilty of a variety of crimes. Some of these rolled-up sheets of lead with scratched messages have recently been found at Bath and they include references to thefts of a hooded cloak, a silver ring and a bronze vessel, while another, also from Bath, curses a long list of

Writing tablet from Vindolanda. The thin leaf of wood has an inscription written in ink, one of a series from this site which provides a fascinating insight into everyday life in a Roman fort.

people responsible for the loss of a girl called Vilbia. Was this an ancient kidnap, or had her friends and relations persuaded her to turn against her lover?

All of this leaves us with a feeling that we are very close to Roman Britain. Indeed, the sympathy felt for the Romans has sometimes led to close parallels being drawn between the British and Roman Empires, even to the extent of almost claiming the Romans as twentieth-century Britons (just as the eighteenth-century anti-quarian, Stukeley, ended up almost claiming that the Druids were essentially early Anglicans). It is certainly true that for a while Roman remains were seen to be the best training ground for British archaeologists. Although doubts have since arisen as to whether putting trenches through stone forts in the north of England in the rain is really the best preparation for ploughing through mud-brick tells in the Middle East, or for plunging into a tropical rain forest, this policy did seem to work after a fashion at first. Many historical novels set in Roman Britain have also added to a sense of familiarity, and have indeed been the inspiration for more than one professional archaeological career.

Yet the picture of how the invasion happened and what its effects were is still a little obscure. If we are to have any hope of understanding prehistoric society, and which, if any, changes are to be attributed to invasion, we surely need to be able to understand so well documented an invasion as that of the Romans. But do we? Was there a large influx of Italians, homesick for the Mediterranean and sorely in need of presents of warm underpants, who drove out or enslaved a small native population? Or was it the local population who were rapidly transformed from hairy Celts to clean-shaven toga-ed Romans, via immersion in hot water at the new municipal baths?

The first view doesn't really have a lot to commend it. The native population was far too large to have been wiped out, and the foreign influx could never have been more than a small minority. What is more, apart from high-ranking officers and governors in the early days, both army and administration were drawn from all over the Empire, including Britain itself. The Empire was a polyglot institution, apparently without any prejudice against different peoples. Even the emperors were often not Italian: Trajan (AD 98–117) was a Spaniard, as was his successor, Hadrian, of Wall fame. The legions were originally raised in Italy, but the auxiliaries were provincials, and by the later years of the Empire both regular and mosaics, painted wall plaster, stucco and marble mouldings, and a bath suite, had been constructed. Then, around AD 75, this was incorporated into a new and far more magnificent palace. Ranges of rooms surrounded a courtyard, entered through an impressive entrance hall with a fountain. In the courtyard was a formal garden and in the rooms there were fine mosaic floors. The whole thing was on a scale unprecedented for Britain and not easily paralleled outside Italy. Before the palace was built the site was levelled by dumping hundreds of cubic feet of clay and gravel onto the southern and eastern parts. I vividly remember spending three weeks one hot August picking and shovelling that clay and gravel out again, from perfectly cut square trenches, the sides levelled with a spirit level every tea break. Our team worked so hard we had a half-serious offer of employment from the foreman of a group of workmen digging a more mundane hole with traditional lack of enthusiasm on the other side of the road. At least, the girls in the team were working – I seem to remember there was a Frenchman who spent most of his time sitting in a wheelbarrow expounding 'La méthode Wheeler' (digging in square trenches) to visitors. Had he but known it, this system of digging was even then being discarded. So I sympathize with the British slaves who had to put all that earth there in the first place.

This palace has been associated with a man called Cogidubnus, a native king who used to be claimed as the only British Roman senator, an amazing honour if true, but maybe mistakenly attributed to him. It is also not entirely certain, though plausible, that he was the owner of Fishbourne. He must have lived to a ripe old age if he was, as he would have had to have been active from the AD 40s through to the 80s. It is also possible that this was the seaside palace of a high-ranking army officer or administrator.

It was certainly built by foreign craftsmen according to Mediterranean models, and was not entirely suitable for northern climates. The earlier mosaics are in a chilly black and white and in the original design there was no provision for heating in many of the rooms, so that braziers had to be brought in to combat the cold, which damaged some of those expensive floors. If this place was built for a native ruler and not for a foreign official, it was a most lavish reward for whatever services he had offered to the Romans, and a most impressive sign of how quickly and thoroughly a Briton could become a Roman. Though I expect his family might have missed their cosy wooden hut with its warm fire as they crouched over some of those braziers in the cool rooms of their fine new palace.

Excavation of the Roman spring at Bath, focus of a great temple complex which underlies the Pump Room.

At Bath, also, enough survives to recreate the past. The steaming water of the Great Bath still looks fairly inviting, despite some scum around the edges, but I resisted any suggestion that I should say my piece to camera whilst swimming. Barry Cunliffe has recently excavated in Bath, down a very hot and steamy hole made all the more alarming by the fact that the work had been occasioned by the discovery that the waters were dangerously infected. The digging was accompanied by all the paraphernalia of disinfection, with

special clothing, masks and so on. The results were very interesting, and showed how the original hot spring, sacred to a Celtic deity, Sul, had been walled in and incorporated into a Roman bath and temple complex. Part of the temple precinct was also excavated and can now be seen beneath the Pump Room.

Baths in any Roman town were an important part of the social life of the citizens. They were places for exercise and relaxation, for meeting friends and even for listening to philosophers. At Bath there was the added attraction of the curative powers of the water. People came here for a cure, as they did in later centuries, and they also retired here. Tombstones show that some at least benefited from the waters to live to a ripe old age – at least one retired soldier was over eighty when he died and there was a seventy-five-year-old priest with a much younger wife.

Civilized and quintessentially Roman though baths may be, at Bath they were built over a spring which had been sacred in prehistoric times to the god or goddess Sul, only partially disguised by later bracketing with Minerva. The Roman name of the place, Aquae Sulis, commemorates the Iron Age and not the Roman deity.

From some points of view, Romanitas descended like a blanket over Britain for four centuries, and from archaeological evidence alone one might be justified in imagining there was a huge invasion and a folk migration. Yet we know there was no immigration on a large scale, and that much of the existing population survived. On the one hand the Roman conquest is a model for the successful imposition of a new way of life by a well-organized government with an effective army. It shows how a minority can dramatically affect the majority, even down to the language spoken, in some levels of society, and the shape of the cooking pots. This conclusion must give us pause before interpreting changes in pot styles in prehistory as signalling major changes in population. On the other hand, at the end of those four centuries, much of Roman culture seems to have disappeared with remarkable speed and completeness. From some points of view, nothing was left but a taste for Mediterranean wine, which prehistoric chiefs had already acquired anyway, while ways of organizing society, economy, and art in the post-Roman centuries appear very similar to those of the pre-Roman period, to the extent that it can be difficult to distinguish between the two on excavated sites. So was the conquest really so complete as it looks?

In the first place, we should remember why the Romans came. The details have been given often before, so I shall not repeat them here, but the main stimulus seems to have been both economic and political. There may have been a need to protect Gaul from a potentially hostile Britain, or to keep a large army occupied in the days when the Empire was still expanding. The grain and minerals of the islands may have been attractive, partly as potential sources of supply for the army. But the political ambitions of generals, and the need for emperors to acquire glory in foreign conquest to bolster their position at home, may have been far more crucial. The history of the invasion and the subsequent fortunes of the province are bound up with the varying interests of successive Roman leaders. Julius Caesar was able to turn his rather inconclusive or even unsuccessful expeditions across the Channel to good political advantage in Rome. Caligula wondered whether Britain might not be a useful diversion from other activities, like murdering his relations, and Claudius finally decided that the best way of consolidating his own position was by conquest of a land beyond the end of the world. He actually appeared to lead the army himself, once victory had been assured. Later, Hadrian's visits provoked considerable activity, though the tendency to attribute all possible developments of the early second century to him should be resisted. Throughout the centuries of Roman rule there was an ebb and flow of military forces and resources as Britain was alternately drained of troops to support some imperial candidate in his struggle for power, or to protect some other part of the Empire, or instead had to be sorted out after some barbarian incursion.

The military character of the conquest is as clear as the political, though its expression changed. Initially the occupying army planted forts to suppress the natives, but later massive defences, city walls and frontier works, were built to protect the citizens of a Roman province. Much of this cannot be understood by reference to Britain alone, as what happened to this peripheral part of a large empire was the result of policies with far wider implications. The Romans were not here from zeal to civilize barbarians, but for their own purposes.

We have to decide what kind of effect the implantation of a large army, originally entirely foreign, had on the local population. The visible remains are still dramatic. There are the roads, miles and miles of them, some buried under modern roads which still take the same route, others only visible from the air, where they can be seen driving straight across fields, or preserved as boundary lines or trackways. Some original stretches of road are still visible today, like the paved way at Wade's Causeway in Yorkshire. The gravelled

some form of control over the land immediately to the north probably remained even when it was not officially part of the province. The wall was a visible symbol of power, to prevent natives to north and south forgetting who was in control – it was also useful for controlling traffic in both directions, as everything had to go through the gates, where tolls could be charged. It would have prevented cattle-raiding, and patrols along it would have had good warning of imminent raids, but it was not designed to cut off communication entirely.

Why was it built anyway? In fact the Wall represents a failure of the original imperial expansionist aims. In the early days of the Empire the armies kept winning new lands, the boundaries kept expanding and the idea of a permanent fixed frontier, a limit to the Empire, would have been unthought of. The fact that Agricola's campaigns to the far north of Scotland were not followed up, still less his optimistic idea of the feasibility of conquering Ireland with a single legion, is a sign of the beginning of the end, that the Empire had begun to run out of steam. Agricola was recalled in AD 84 or 85 and by AD 122, less than forty years later, Hadrian could see a frontier which ran to the south of all modern Scotland as not only a good solution to the British problem, but also a way of enhancing his own reputation. And that is quite possibly why the Wall was built – unless Hadrian really had heard of the Great Wall of China as has recently been partly seriously suggested. Instead of winning great victories and adding lands to the Empire, he could gain glory by building a wall to keep the barbarians at bay. The grandiose plan for a massive stone wall and mathematically laid out fortlets may have been his, modified in the face of practicalities. Only someone who had drawn up a plan in an office, with an eye more to show than to strategy, would have insisted on building a wall on top of a cliff, still less on putting gates which opened onto that cliff, a route useful only for goats and mountaineers.

Hadrian may have had something to do with a quite different project, which, although apparently civilian, has a certain military flavour to it. This was the construction of a new town in the east of England, at Stonea, near March. Here Tim Potter from the British Museum excavated a site which was probably built at a time when the fens were more densely occupied than they were to be again until recent centuries. Earthworks of many Roman villages used to exist in this area, until they fell victim to ploughing. Sea-level may have been lower than it is now, but the Romans also carried out massive

Reconstruction of the tower at Stonea, Cambridgeshire, based partly on a surviving tower at Anguillara, near Rome.

drainage operations. The Car Dyke, which they constructed, was once thought to have been a canal, but now looks like a series of discontinuous ditches, useful for drainage but not for transport. The site at Stonea may have been planned as the administrative centre of imperial estates in this newly occupied region, and it may have been another of Hadrian's bright ideas, as it was founded during his reign, in the first half of the second century.

The most dramatic find was the massive foundations of a great stone tower. It has been possible to draw an attractive picture of what this might have looked like, complete with dog, because a parallel is known, which survives to well above foundation level. This is a tower at Anguillara in Italy, north of Rome. If this comparison is correct, it is an extraordinary example of the translation of a building plan from the heart of the Empire to its fringe. A stone tower rising out of the flat fenland must have dominated the landscape, as Ely cathedral has done since. The villagers would have known where to go to pay their taxes and to bring goods to market – though they might have had as much difficulty in travelling directly over the fens then as now, where the dykes usually frustrate any direct approaches. Another odd feature of Stonea was an enormous pit, full of the wet wood so beloved of archaeologists, including some very interesting things, such as pitchforks, a spade, planks, buckets and pieces of furniture. When

*The basilica at·
Silchester viewed from
the north. The north
range with traces of an
early apse can be seen at
the bottom of the photo.
The pitted floor of the
basilica is caused by
metalworking activity
and Victorian
excavation.*

A Victorian navvy, and those in charge of him, might not have been able to miss a stone wall or a mosaic, but they were not attuned to post-holes. Fortunately, they do not seem to have succeeded in removing all the evidence, as Mike Fulford, from Reading, has been finding out. Not only are the layers beneath buildings still intact as one might have expected, but much later evidence was not removed. The forum and basilica excavation is proving especially interesting.

The basilica was probably something like a town hall and a law court, although, like other terms used casually in relation to Roman Britain, the meaning of the word in this context is not really entirely clear. The Silchester basilica was built in the early years of the second century, when the local authorities constructed a magnificent building to replace an earlier timber structure. No expense was spared – there were stone columns with Corinthian capitals and painted plaster, and the marble used had come not only from

Purbeck but had also been imported from the Mediterranean. Yet before the middle of the third century this imposing structure had been converted into a row of workshops. The marble hall had been partitioned with wooden walls into a series of small rooms, and these were full of the rubbish associated with metalworking, first bronze and later iron. The fact that the rooms are all about the same size, and that their occupants all seem to have been carrying out the same kind of work, changing from bronze- to iron-working together, suggests some continuing official control, but metalworking is hardly the kind of activity one would imagine in such a place. Those, like myself, brought up on Rosemary Sutcliffe's *The Eagle of the Ninth* will not be enthusiastic about the idea that a battered eagle found at Silchester was simply part of a consignment of scrap, due for melting down – but it is an explanation that does fit the facts. Especially since it is not now thought that the ninth legion disappeared in Scotland. . . .

So the civic centre of a flourishing town was given over to craftsmen. Maybe official business was moved elsewhere because the basilica could no longer be maintained in the style for which it had been designed, and had become too expensive to repair. But there are other indications that towns did not maintain their initial impetus into the third and fourth centuries. At many urban sites excavators have encountered a phenomenon known as the black earth, a boring deposit of fairly barren dark soil, lying on top of Roman levels and underneath late Saxon or medieval deposits. Analysis seems to show that this soil had been cultivated, though it is not always clear whether this means there were large fields inside the walls, or just garden plots. Some of the soil may have been deliberately dumped, or it may have accumulated over time. The obvious explanation, which may hold true for some places, is that this deposit represents the abandonment of towns during the fifth century. Those who are keen to find life in towns during the early Saxon period used to search those layers of black earth desperately for signs of Saxon huts or pottery, usually with little success. Recently it has become clear that at least some of this soil accumulated much earlier. In London excavations within the walled area of the city have shown that very little was happening after the second century to the west of the Walbrook. On top of buildings occupied in the second century there is earth, some apparently deliberately dumped there after the houses had been demolished. At Southwark, on the other side of the Thames, the same thing of surfaces could wear down and be replaced very quickly, to be succeeded by several phases of timber buildings, then everything at Wroxeter could be squeezed into the first half of the fifth century. On the other hand, you might think that it takes a fair time for feet to wear down paved roads, and Philip Barker points out that visitors' feet have not yet made much impression on the part of the city which has been laid out for them to walk over for some years now.

At Wroxeter the sequence seems to be that the large basilica building at one side of the baths was demolished early in the fourth century, except for the dramatic bit of wall known as 'The Old Work' (which the camera dwelt on most of the time the commentary was talking about fragile traces of timber buildings). A series of small wooden buildings was built, and then swept away before the whole area was covered with fine rubble. This rubble consisted of the finely sifted, ground-up remains of buildings, and whoever had it brought in and laid down could mobilize a reasonable amount of labour. He also had grandiose ideas, since a large and imposing timber house was then constructed, with two storeys and classical porticoes. Clearly, there was still some idea of maintaining a 'Roman' style of life. Wroxeter may have been a slightly odd place, as one of the main finds has been numerous plaster and metal objects in the shape of eyes. There are also skulls which have been treated with oil – all very odd and un-Roman, in contrast with the building. We don't know whether the porticoed house was the focus of a small settled nucleus within the old walls, like a chief's palace or fort, or whether we should think in terms of similar late occupation over other parts of the town. Since it has taken so long to get so far with one part of the site, I don't expect we shall know about the rest for years, if ever: it isn't the kind of information you can get in a hurry.

There is a question-mark over the end of Roman towns, therefore. Some evidence points towards an early abandonment and to the fact that urbanism did not develop a solid base amongst the native population, whilst at Wroxeter we have a suggestion that life in that town may have gone on far longer than might have been expected. On the Continent the picture is sometimes clearer than in Britain, since in some places rather more substantial remains have been preserved. But even then, the story is not always straightforward.

For example, Trier, which lies not far from the Rhine frontier of the Empire, by a crossing of the River Moselle, was the capital of part of the Empire in the fourth century. Constantine the Great was responsible for some of the buildings which can be seen today. The

The Porta Nigra *at Trier, on the banks of the Moselle in West Germany. The Roman gate was preserved by its conversion into a medieval church.*

survival of masonry from the Roman period is considerable: parts of the city walls were incorporated into the medieval circuit, the piers of the bridge are Roman, there are parts of two bath complexes, one so large you can get lost in the maze of drains which are high enough for people to be able to walk along them upright, and almost the whole of the north gate. There is the amphitheatre, part of the cathedral and a large building called the basilica attached incongruously to part of a pink rococo palace. Here it really does look was probably in such places that the La Tène art styles revived and where such things as the bronze enamelled escutcheons of hanging bowls were made, or the penannular brooches, named from their broken ring-shape. The masterpieces of metalwork and manuscript illumination which were to be made in early Christian Britain emerged from this tradition, which had somehow reappeared after four centuries of Roman rule.

In the west at least it is possible to argue for a view of Roman Britain as a transient passing phase, which left people much the same afterwards as they were before. It is also clear that there were people there in the post-Roman centuries, people who were descended from the previous inhabitants with perhaps a few traces of Romanitas grafted onto their prehistoric lifestyle. In the east of England it has been thought that there was a much more dramatic change, and an extinction of much that had gone before, with the arrival of the Anglo-Saxons, the subject of the next chapter.

Chapter 5

Seawolves and Saints

The end of Roman Britain has often been seen as a drama involving the irruption of barbarian hordes into a country left undefended and partly empty by the withdrawal of the Romans. The story goes that the British King Vortigern, left to fend for himself, asked in some Germanic barbarians to help him against the Picts. These arrived in three ships, led by Hengest and Horsa, but soon turned upon the Britons themselves and overran the country with fire and the sword until 'flames licked the land from sea to sea and the cities ran with blood'. Despite later heroic efforts by Ambrosius Aurelianus, the Britons went under, dead, enslaved or lurking in the Welsh mountains, and the Anglo-Saxons took over much of lowland England, giving it its native language and probably much of its present appearance and people. Or, in archaeological terms, there was a great crash of falling masonry and breaking pottery as the legions sailed away into the sunset, leaving a few poor natives to scratch about in the ruins before being overwhelmed.

This version of events has been given by most writers since Bede, who wrote in the eighth century, and it underlies even the most sophisticated analyses of the period. Yet it all depends on one early historical source, written by someone whose own terms of reference were so imprecise that we don't know when or where he was writing, what his own occupation was, nor when or where most of the events he describes took place. Most historians have been a little more optimistic than that, and would say that the author of *The Ruin of Britain* was a monk called Gildas, writing in Britain during the sixth century. And a great deal of ink has been spilled in attempts to reconcile the various contradictory dates for events in the fifth century which can be extracted from this work.

*View of one corner of
the late Roman fort at
Burgh Castle, Norfolk.*

Within Britain claims have been made for evidence of disaster, such as burnt-down villas and buildings in towns and bodies thrown down wells. Some of this may well reflect war or plague, but exactly which episode of destruction, from 367 onwards, or even earlier, is represented in each case, is seldom clear. And the burning of a building could just as well have been the result of an ordinary domestic fire. Fire was always a hazard with timber buildings and even with stone-built houses, where the stoke-hole for the heating could get out of control. Bodies are also difficult to interpret. Those found in old excavations may have been interpreted as unburied, when in fact they were lying in ordinary graves whose edges were simply not detected.

Burying hoards of gold and silver is usually seen as a sign of instability, and there are a number of hoards from southern England of fourth- and fifth-century date. Again, the general pattern is suggestive, but each individual hoard might be explained in other terms. The most famous metalwork hoards, such as the Water Newton and Thetford treasures, may have religious explanations. The Water Newton silver objects have been described as 'the first Christian Church plate' and they might have been buried at a time of persecution, while the pagan character of some of the gold objects found at Thetford might suggest that in this case it was the guardians of a pagan temple who felt insecure. The Thetford treasure could also be interpreted as the stock of a jeweller, buried for safe keeping, perhaps indeed because of raiders.

Exactly when Roman buildings went out of use, if they were not burnt down, is not always easy to determine, as we have seen at Wroxeter, and might have been long after the latest datable object. Roman roof tiles collapsed onto a layer of earth containing late Saxon pottery in a building in York, and others might have lasted as long. Traces of timber buildings above more solid stone foundations could well have been lost, or not be practicably recoverable in the small holes which are often all there is to dig in an urban context.

Yet, when all allowances have been made, there clearly was an end to the Roman way of life, and typically 'Roman' kinds of archaeological evidence disappear. In the west they are replaced, as we have seen, by something very like an impoverished version of Iron Age society – but in the east the story is very different. In place of stone-built houses with tiled roofs and plastered walls, there are timber huts and pits full of rubbish. In place of burials laid out in coffins with only the odd pot or coin to accompany the corpse, there

are graves equipped with jewellery and weapons, many of them cremations in hand-made pots. It is easy to find parallels across the North Sea, in the Netherlands, Germany and Denmark.

At the museum in Schleswig Holstein, a romantic castle with a moat, there are collections of finds from cemeteries and settlements of the first to fifth centuries, the 'Roman Iron Age' in Continental terminology, since these lands never became part of the Empire. Burial was chiefly by cremation, with the bones often collected up afterwards and put in a pot, along with fragments of the metalwork attached to the clothes the body had been burnt in. Other odds and ends of equipment found in such pots perhaps included objects deliberately deposited as part of the funeral ritual – sets of miniature shears, tweezers and amulets, and charms such as animal tusks or claws. Some of the metalwork was made within the Empire and the decoration on the pots can sometimes be traced to Roman glass or silverware designs. Roman objects were no doubt prized loot, but they also arrived in the course of trade, or as gifts to secure assistance against other less friendly tribes. And since many Germanic tribesmen were recruited into the Roman army, when they went home they would have taken with them many things acquired while on service. Roman design influenced Germanic craftsmen and throughout the fifth and sixth centuries we can see how what was once a straightforward classical design was changed in the hands of a Germanic craftsman. A four-legged beast crouching along the edge of a buckle plate becomes a wild and convoluted tangle of disjointed animal bodies and limbs, with the odd human face or hand, derived from representations of emperors or gods. For some reason, while the Celtic craftsmen created abstract curvilinear patterns with occasional fairly naturalistic animal or human heads, Germanic society, which may not have been so very unlike Celtic, produced this very different art. The preoccupation with animals, often so unrecognizable as to be almost codified, goes right through into Viking art.

At Schleswig and in Denmark we can even see what some of the people looked like, from the bog burials. The hair and skin of some of these corpses is so well preserved it is no wonder early finds by peat cutters were reported as recent murders, or thought to be drunks who had drowned when they fell in the bog. Some are clearly ancient murders, or execution victims, strangled or with their throats cut. Our only recent British find, 'Pete Marsh', or 'Lindow man', from Cheshire, was garotted: since he seems to belong to the

The body of a young Iron Age girl buried in a bog in Schleswig Holstein, West Germany.

pre-Roman Iron Age, and since other examples of bog burials have in fact been reported from the British Isles, we cannot regard it as a purely Germanic habit to dump bodies in lakes or bogs, whether privately murdered or publicly executed or sacrificed. These bodies do take us very close to prehistoric people – though the reconstruction of one girl as a very modern blonde might be taken with a pinch of salt, as she ended up looking very like a girl who had recently been murdered at the time the reconstruction was being made.

The historical accounts of sea pirates make it clear that these were accomplished seamen, but the Nydam boat, also preserved at Schleswig, is an actual example of one of their ships. It is a large rowing boat which could certainly have made the sea-crossing over the North Sea, perhaps by way of a long route along the coast before striking out across the Channel, or over the North Sea to East Anglia and down one of the main rivers inland.

The large collections of weapons, found especially in bogs, are witness to warfare and unrest, while Germanic love of fighting is abandonment during the fifth century. This site, like many others, consists of a flat featureless piece of ground, covered with the marks of post-holes. At first it looks like a hopelessly confused muddle, but the orderly minds of modern Germanic excavators can disentangle the orderly house and village plans of their ancestors.

The houses were long rectangular timber buildings, often with living quarters for humans at one end and stalls for cattle at the other. The waterlogged foundations from the terp sites have filled out the details of houses like this, so that they can be reconstructed. There was a fireplace for cooking in the living end and wooden or wattlework partitions dividing up the cattle stalls at the other end, with perhaps a third section in some houses which was used as a barn or workshop. Sometimes several buildings were grouped together in square fenced enclosures, and the enclosures lay along a street. Overall, the villages present a remarkably uniform appearance, whether in Denmark, north Germany or the Netherlands, with houses laid out all in the same direction in tidy rows. Sometimes there seems to have been one house rather larger than the others, with perhaps more associated workshops or granaries. I suppose this might have been something like a village hall, or some communal focus, but such large houses are usually interpreted as chiefs' residences and are seen as a sign of the growth of a hierarchical society. In the later phases there were also small structures known as grubenhäuser, or pit houses.

Structures of this type are the most obvious sign of the arrival of immigrants in England. 'Pit houses' full of Anglo-Saxon pottery and food bones were for a long time the main features recognized on settlement sites. They were seen as dug-outs, the nasty primitive homes of the nasty primitive barbarians. The idea was that a sort of tent roof was built over the pit, within which the Anglo-Saxons lived amidst the debris of their meals, along with dead dogs and perhaps live pigs, in utter filth and squalor. However, while it is true that they do not seem to have been obsessed with washing, the Anglo-Saxons were not a primitive people. They were skilled metalworkers and they must also have been experienced in carpentry and building in timber, since their ancestors had been constructing large wooden houses for centuries, to say nothing of boats. Crossing the North Sea should not have caused them to forget how to build, and in fact excavations in recent decades have shown they did not.

At West Stow, near Bury St Edmunds in Suffolk, Stanley West excavated most of an Anglo-Saxon village, occupied from the early

Reconstructed Anglo-Saxon houses at West Stow, Suffolk. The one in the foreground has probably been built with a slightly over-tall roof.

fifth to the seventh centuries. In the days when it was being excavated, this was not a very lovely place: part of it had been a sewage farm and the municipal rubbish tip loomed across the heath, advancing towards the site, which it was scheduled to engulf. Digging there was quite exciting: you never knew whether you might not find a rat (of the four-legged variety) in your sleeping bag, or helping itself to some of the eternal seething curry favoured by one supervisor. Nowadays West Stow is very salubrious, landscaped into a country park with grass and trees and the site of the village preserved. Some of the houses have been reconstructed, and others are still being built, so there are heaps of wood chips and hewn logs spread about.

There were two kinds of building at West Stow, the grubenhäuser or sunken-featured buildings, SFBs for short, and rectangular post-

Different reconstructions of an Anglo-Saxon building based on the same excavated evidence from an Anglo-Saxon settlement at Cowdery's Down, near Basingstoke, Hampshire, excavated by Martin Millett.

buildings might really have been covered with decoration with all sorts of carved gables and ornamented doorposts.

The Cowdery's Down building is comparable with some of the timber halls excavated at Yeavering, near Wooler in Northumberland. Nowadays there is nothing to see at Yeavering, just an empty field below a hillfort. But air photographs showed the field was full of the foundations of wooden buildings, which were excavated by Brian Hope-Taylor some years ago. This was probably the place called 'Ad Gefrin' where King Edwin had a palace, according to Bede, and where Paulinus preached Christianity, perhaps from the curious structure like a segment of an amphitheatre, only built in wood, which was found there. Air photographs have shown up similar structures elsewhere, which may also have been Saxon palaces, though we should remember that one at least of these, Balbridie, turned out to be Neolithic.

So the Anglo-Saxons did not lose their ability to build in wood when they left their homelands. But they do seem to have left some things behind. The typical long house, with animal stalls and human living quarters combined under one roof, does not appear in England. Maybe in the English climate it was not necessary to keep animals indoors over the winter, and the more fertile land meant there was less need to collect every scrap of dung for manure, but it is surprising that the immigrants realized this so soon. The use of aisle posts, which meant a roof could be spanned without needing very long timbers, might also have been given up because better, longer timbers were available in England, but it is again surprising that the Anglo-Saxons changed at once to a new building method. The classic English Anglo-Saxon house is a rectangle, a near double square, with opposed doors in the middle of the long sides and a narrow partition at one end. This is not a continental type. And the villages in England are rarely so tidy as those on the Continent: the houses straggle and cluster and only occasionally do we see the neat rectangularity found across the North Sea.

All these features suggest we should look more carefully at the antecedents of Anglo-Saxon buildings, and not automatically assume that they are simply a translation of Germanic ideas onto British soil. Some features could have originated amongst the native Britons. It might be worth looking more carefully at the ordinary rural buildings of Roman Britain, rather than the more upper-class villas, to see if some of that building tradition has been passed on. If so, it might affect our ideas about the relationship between Briton and Saxon. You don't learn how to build a house from a corpse.

The change in burial rites looks more clear-cut. Late Roman burial practice involved largely unaccompanied inhumation. Bodies may have been buried in a shroud, or sometimes in clothes, since the nails from their boots remain, but they usually did not have any, or many, objects in the grave with them. This practice may have been partly due to Christian teaching, although it is not clear that Christianity automatically precludes the burial of grave-goods. Certainly in later centuries some very rich burials were of Christians, and even Saint Cuthbert had a variety of things put in his coffin. Anglo-Saxon burials, on the other hand, both on the Continent and in England, were very often accompanied by a large number of objects, and many were cremations, not inhumations. All over southeastern England cemeteries have been found, and are still being found every year. Many of the hundreds of sites, it is true, are known only from casual records and from a handful of finds in the local museum. Others have been excavated on a larger scale, although all too few of these have been published and in many cases the burials recovered were only part of a cemetery, the rest long since destroyed by gravel quarries, roads, or buildings. They do attract attention because of the finds: large flashy bronze brooches and beads in female graves, iron spears, shields and swords buried with

Burnt objects found with
cremated bones in a pot
at Spong Hill. These
include a pair of round
saucer brooches (1),
part of a larger equal-
armed brooch (2), a
silver finger ring (3),
part of a bone comb (4)
and a spindle-whorl (5).

remains which appear to tell us that from the middle of the fifth century we are dealing with something quite new, a break with what had gone before as Britain became England.

I do not myself think that is the whole picture. If we go back again to the story of Hengest and Horsa, we do find that at first plenty of archaeological evidence appears to confirm it. The presence of Germanic soldiers in Britain, we are told, is clearly demonstrated by the distribution of later Roman military belt-fittings around the country. These buckles and strap ends are part of a series which is found all over the Empire, especially clustered along the Rhine and Danube frontiers where one would expect the army to have been. They are often elaborately decorated, in styles which were to be taken up and developed later by Germanic craftsmen.

Since there were many Germanic soldiers in the army, who could have taken such things home (as we know they did), where native craftsmen could have copied them, this does not lend the belt fittings themselves any 'Germanic' character. There seems no reason to doubt that these items were part of the equipment of the regular army, and no very good reason to suggest that they were issued only to irregular barbarian troops, federates or mercenaries as they have been called. In any case, some pieces may have arrived in the ground long after they had been made, and may by then have been heirlooms or loot, no longer in military ownership at all. Some of the most attractive late Roman buckles found in Britain are small and delicate, with pairs of horses' heads on the loop and incised patterns on the plates, including pairs of peacocks with a tree of life, interpreted as Christian symbols. These do not look at all military, and indeed have been found in female graves. I do not think the distribution pattern of late Roman buckles in Britain should be used to plot the location of barbarian troops, or to reconstruct Vortigern's strategy against the Picts. The evidence simply will not go that far, and all we have is an interesting class of metalwork which can give an approximate date of the late fourth century or later to whatever context it is found in. But it is not proof of the existence of Hengest and Horsa or anyone like them.

Even the considerable archaeological visibility of the Anglo-Saxons, in other words the fact that their houses and burials have been found all over eastern England, should be treated with some caution. It could be that not all that looks Anglo-Saxon really is so, and it could also be that the archaeological record is a bit misleading, and that the visibility of certain kinds of people, or at least evidence for them, is obscuring our picture of the fifth and sixth centuries. Could some of the 'Saxons' really have been Britons? Or were there a lot of Britons still living in England who have left little or no traces? Neither of these ideas is unreasonable, but neither is easy to demonstrate.

One way to investigate this might be through the skeletons of the people themselves. If one could show either a dramatic change in physical type, or, alternatively, continuity, one would have a sound basis for argument. Unfortunately the soil of East Anglia, where many of the cemeteries have been found, includes a lot of glacial sands and gravels which are too acid to preserve bones, apart from the odd tooth or jawbone preserved by chemicals from nearby bronze objects. Stains in the soil, showing where a body once was, can sometimes be seen. At Sutton Hoo they have even managed to excavate such stains in three dimensions, producing 'sand-persons'. But this does not allow for the fine examination of bone details which might allow comparisons between the physical characteristics of natives and immigrants. There are quantities of cremated bones, but these really are not conducive to such studies either.

Bones from other parts of England survive better, but these seem far too often to have fallen victim to the 'unpublished report syndrome', which bedevils archaeology in general and Anglo-Saxon cemeteries in particular. I have heard it said that it is possible to detect alien male burials in southern England, but not female. If so, this would perhaps be a sign that Germanic soldiers were coming and settling, then marrying local girls rather than bringing their own womenfolk and families with them. The best-preserved skull at Spong Hill has been said to look like earlier local skulls, which might indicate a similar pattern there, since this was a female skeleton. But I think the quantity of Germanic jewellery in England must argue for the arrival of some foreign women, even if the metalwork was soon copied by the locals. It is probably unrealistic to think that a 'Germanic' type can be confidently distinguished from a 'British' type of skeleton, but if long-lived large cemeteries could be looked at in detail some kind of pattern should emerge, so that one could see if and when there were breaks and changes. There are as yet no studies of this kind published in England, but something like this has been done in France.

At Frènouville in Normandy a cemetery was excavated by Christian Pilet, whom we filmed digging a settlement site of a similar period. The burials at Frènouville dated from the third to the

Late Roman military belt fittings from Dorchester on Thames, Oxfordshire.

from the Continent where the workshops had not gone out of action. There might, however, be other kinds of object which would repay further study. All sorts of odd things, such as animal claws or teeth, cowrie shells, lumps of crystal and other stones, occur in graves. These are loosely described as 'amulets', and they may well have had some religious or magical significance. It would be interesting to see whether the pattern of such finds looks like the pattern found in continental Germanic graves, or whether it finds echoes in Romano-British customs and therefore provides another thread in the search for the native population. There is also the possibility I have already mentioned that some features of Anglo-Saxon buildings derive from native building traditions. So there are several potential lines of enquiry, none as yet fully worked out, in the search for possible Britons disguised as Anglo-Saxons.

Another possibility is that the British population did partly survive in areas settled by Saxons, but that they kept themselves to themselves and did not mix with the immigrants. If so, they might not be very visible in the archaeological record. If we consider how difficult it is to identify post-Roman settlement in the west, where sites have been so diligently sought in the quest for Arthur, and where there is no Anglo-Saxon 'noise' to confuse the issue, how much more difficult is it likely to be to find them in the east. But they might, nonetheless, have been there.

Some late Roman villas and parts of towns seem to have continued in use long after the latest datable coins or pottery, and the same might be true of many more. The old buildings would have been patched up for as long as possible and then replaced by timber building in an idiom it would be hard to describe as either British or Saxon. People may have largely dispensed with pottery, or made hand-made pots, partly copying their new neighbours, partly perhaps going back to their own old traditions, once good wheel-thrown pots could no longer be bought at market. Collapse of the production and distribution networks of a complex society often means the survivors are forced back into much more primitive ways of doing things, because there had been specialists before, so most people didn't know how to make good pots.

We are not likely to identify the burials of these people, assuming they existed, if they were continuing the Roman habit of burial without grave-goods. In the west, despite this difficulty, a few such cemeteries have been found. For example, there was one at Cannington in Somerset where the very few grave-goods, combined with carbon-14, allow a tentative third- to eighth-century dating. Such a cemetery, found in the east of England, could well have been written off as late Roman or medieval, especially if there had been even fewer associated objects. Perhaps we should also remember all the many graves in Anglo-Saxon cemeteries which do not have grave-goods, and which are usually written off as belonging to slaves, or as the latest burials from a time when the practice of grave-goods was going out, even amongst pagans. Some of these graves, however, might also be those of the local native British population.

Two ways of approaching the subject which seem to have been producing some results lately are through the techniques of field survey and topographical analysis. Aerial photography has dramatically changed our view of past landscapes, but it is only useful for certain soils under certain conditions, in particular light

When, in later centuries, the peoples of south and eastern England called themselves Angles or Saxons, we have to allow for the possibility that this may not have represented a straightforward ethnic fact. Bede, writing in the eighth century, was sure of his own Englishness – at least, he seems very unenthusiastic about the Britons. But there is little evidence for mass migration, even on conventional terms, north of York. Bede was writing at Jarrow in Northumbria, where the ruling dynasty, and their immediate following, may well have been Angles. But the rest of the population were probably of British descent, who, however, identified with their rulers, either willingly or because it was prudent to do so. The sense of belonging to a particular area, East Anglia or Sussex, Northumbria or Kent, would have increased as time went by. Some of these regional identities may have had even older roots: the similarity I have already noted between Iron Age and Anglo-Saxon tribal divisions may not be entirely coincidental, nor entirely dictated by geography. And of course many areas we now think of as 'English', like Somerset and the west Midlands, were not even nominally Anglo-Saxon until long after the first migrations.

Chapter 6 | Raiders or Traders?

In the year 793 Viking raiders attacked the monastery on Lindisfarne, burial place of St Cuthbert. Alcuin of York heard of the catastrophe in France, and wrote anguished letters home: 'never before has such terror appeared in Britain', he wrote, 'the church of St Cuthbert spattered with the blood of the priests of God'. He was fairly clear that the reason for the visitation was the wickedness of the English – the line taken by Gildas three hundred years earlier, except that then, of course, it was the English who were the instrument of God's wrath upon the British, now it was the peaceful Christian English who were being assailed by northern sea pirates. Later chroniclers followed a similar line, as the raids spread around Britain and Ireland, and to France. This was the beginning of what has been called the Viking Age, from the end of the eighth to well into the eleventh century. The popular version of the Vikings has followed that of the chroniclers in seeing them as wholly savage pagan marauders, whose only aim in life was slaughter and pillage, and whose path could be tracked by the smoke of burning churches and the blood of slaughtered Christians. These warriors fought with no fear, since death in battle was the desired end for a Viking, rewarded by eternal feasting in Valhalla.

The familiar picture used to be of a giant, axe-wielding Viking, complete with winged helmet, blood dripping from his moustache and a few captive women slung over his shoulder, appearing from nowhere in his fast ships, and then disappearing with equal speed back to his wild northern homelands. A few years ago a new view of the Viking began to be propagated. It was pointed out that all our historical sources for Viking activity are even more biased than is usually the case, since monastic chroniclers were naturally especially appalled by the pagan Vikings' lack of respect for Christian holy also some more extensive settlements, which might even be called towns.

One of these places lay on the island of Birka, in Lake Mälar in central Sweden. Now this is a peaceful place, with only one or two farm buildings, visited mostly by summer tourists or archaeologists. Bare rocks rise out of a thin cover of birch trees, and green pasture runs down to the water's edge. Yet in the ninth and tenth centuries this was a thriving town, a centre for the trade between Sweden and the rest of the world. Amongst the trees you can still see many mounds, grassed-over heaps of stones which mark the burial places of people who lived here then. Over two thousand of these burial mounds have been counted and many were excavated in the last century by Hjalmar Stolpe. Fortunately he was a careful and meticulous archaeologist for his day, who kept a detailed record of his finds.

There are also earth banks surrounding a rocky peak known as the citadel, and cutting off a semi-circular area of land by the shore, the area of the Viking town. The water level was higher in those days so that what is now one island was then two, and there were good harbours by the settlement. Stolpe and others since have cut trenches through the settlement area, but so far no really clear picture of it has been produced.

The region around Lake Mälar has always been the most densely occupied part of Sweden, especially if Skåne, in the south, is excluded on the grounds that for a long time it was part of Denmark. The economic and political focus has always been here, where inland and external trade routes converged. Before Birka became important there was a settlement on another island, Helgö, where considerable evidence for bronze-working has been found, together with imported objects from as far afield as Ireland and even northern India. The medieval centre was at Sigtuna, to the north of the lake, and the present capital, Stockholm, grew up on an island in the middle of the channel which gives access to the lake. In the summer trade was by water, from the Baltic and beyond in one direction, and from inland rivers and lakes to the north in the other. In the winter access was at least as good across the ice. The great natural resources of the thinly populated forests to the north, hides, fur, timber and iron ore, could be brought down and exchanged for foodstuffs and for luxuries.

The burials on Birka include many cremations, the ashes and bones covered by heaps of stones. These are probably the graves of the local population. There are also inhumations, some in large wooden chambers, occasionally with horse skeletons as well as those of humans. There are also burials in ordinary coffins, and others which may have been in dug-out boats. Some bodies were just wrapped in a shroud and put in a hole in the ground. This variety reflects the mixed community of foreign merchants who visited the island, sometimes living and dying there. There were probably some Christians amongst them, since we know there was a Christian missionary, named Ansgar, who spent some time at Birka during the ninth century.

The objects found in the graves include glass and pottery from the Carolingian empire, jewellery from Slavonic countries, and silks from Byzantium or even China. Goods came from all parts of the then-known world, Europe and Asia. The trade routes lay along the North Sea and into the Baltic from western Europe, and up the rivers of Russia from Byzantium and the Arab world. Some of the graves contained scales, needed by merchants for weighing out precious metals. Others had coins, most of which are Islamic. Until the late tenth century far more Arab coins reached Sweden than European, and it is possible that it was disruption of the eastern trade routes which led to increased raids westwards.

The material excavated from the settlement area shows that various crafts were practised there, including metalworking, and the manufacture of bone and leather objects, and also that there was probably a substantial permanent population as well as the fluctuating numbers of visiting merchants. Birka was a rich international community. Yet defences were built in the tenth century and the place did not last long into the eleventh.

Another important trading settlement on the route between Scandinavia and western Europe is the place near modern Schleswig known respectively as Hedeby or Haithabu by Danish and German scholars. Until recent centuries this lay on the Danish side of the border with Germany, but it is now in Schleswig Holstein. The site is now an empty expanse of fields surrounded by a large semi-circular earth bank. Visitors often ask, 'Where is the ancient city?', when they are standing in the middle of it. But this was once a crucial point on a busy trade route.

The Jutland peninsula is notoriously dangerous for shipping, and patterns of wrecks recorded in the nineteenth century show great concentrations around the northwest coast. An alternative and safer route was by land across the narrowest part of the peninsula.

LEFT *Carved wooden bed-head from the ship burial at Oseberg, Norway. The whole object is in the shape of an animal's head and it is also covered with intertwined carved animals.*

RIGHT *The ship excavated at Gokstad in Norway, now in the ship museum at Oslo. A replica of this was made in the nineteenth century soon after it was found and it was sailed from Bergen to Newfoundland in only twenty-eight days.*

production. We have a glimpse of what these may have been like from a burial of about 800, the beginning of the Viking Age. At Oseberg, south of Oslo in Norway, a woman, possibly a queen, was buried in an elaborately carved ship with many other carved objects: beds, sledges, and a cart, all decorated with writhing knots of animals like the metalwork of the time. A tapestry was also preserved, showing a procession of horses and carts with people, the women in long skirts and pigtails and the men with spears. Small metal figures of women like those on the Oseberg tapestry have been found on various Scandinavian sites, and have been interpreted as perhaps possessing religious or cult significance, so perhaps the procession is of gods rather than humans.

The Oseberg ship may not have been designed for long journeys, and was perhaps the possession of a rich woman who used it only for coastal travel. Another ship found at Gokstad, however, was the model for a replica Viking ship which sailed across the Atlantic in 1893 – and for a half-size replica which was incongruously stranded outside the British Museum for a while during the Viking exhibition some years ago. More knowledge of ships has come from a collection which had been deliberately sunk in the entrance to Roskilde harbour, in Denmark, in the eleventh century. These ships were excavated from the shallow waters by surrounding them with a dam and draining the waters inside. Now they are preserved in a museum which sits a bit like a boat on the edge of the water. What is interesting at Roskilde is the variety in the types of ship found there. There were two examples of the famous deadly longship, one larger than the other, a small fishing or ferry boat and two merchant ships. These cargo vessels are broader and slower than the warships, and include one which was perhaps built for long-distance sea journeys and another smaller one for coastal trade.

It was the ships which gave the Scandinavians their key to the rest of the world and it may be that ship-building skills and seamanship had reached a point in the eighth century where it was possible to undertake longer and more dangerous voyages than before. There must have been boats in Scandinavia as long as there have been people there. The earliest known illustrations of boats in fact date to the Bronze Age, but probably these could not have survived very long journeys.

It is possible to write books about the Vikings which concentrate on such things as their houses, art, and skill in woodcarving, with foreign travel thrown in as mostly peaceful trade or exploration. But whole families migrated and settled abroad, and armies, of whatever size, marauded across Britain and Europe for generations. Why did this happen and what was their impact on the countries they attacked?

There is no really clear answer to the first question. The technological ability to build boats, already mentioned, provides only the means, not the cause. Medieval Norse sagas say that it was oppression by kings which drove men from their homes. Centralization of authority under stronger royal dynasties might well have led to conflicts as a result of which the unsuccessful contestants could well have decided to make their fortunes elsewhere. Even more individual reasons may have driven some people: Eric the Red, founder of the Greenland colony, was exiled first from Norway and then from Iceland for violent crimes. There may have been pressure on land, caused either by a rising population or by fluctuations in climate. The realization that the richer and more fertile lands of England and France could be mulcted of their wealth so easily, or even taken over altogether, would have been a magnet for the younger sons of farmers scratching a living in some parts of Scandinavia. This is less true of Denmark, the country of origin of many of those who raided and settled in England, and here the explanation might be better seen in terms of political or population pressure. Eventually, in fact, invasion of England became part of an expansionist, imperial exercise on the part of the Danish kings.

But what was the impact of Viking activity in lands where there were already inhabitants? Did people greet those peaceful traders with open arms and start exchanging goods? Or are the historical accounts of violence, of raids followed by forcible settlement on a large scale, borne out by the archaeological evidence? It might seem surprising that any problems of interpretation would remain, especially for the attacks and settlement in Britain, since the accounts are so detailed. Settlers, mostly of Norwegian origin, colonized the northern islands, the Shetlands, Orkneys and Hebrides and also the Isle of Man. They founded towns in Ireland, of which Dublin is the most famous, and settled in parts of northwestern England. The Danes, on the other hand, overran eastern England, killed the king of East Anglia and took over his kingdom, and also Northumbria and Mercia. They were only prevented from engulfing the whole of England by the heroic efforts of the West Saxon king, Alfred, who forced them to a truce, with an

A Pictish stone house at Buckquoy, Orkney, excavated by Anna Ritchie. The oval, lobed shape is very different from later Norse rectangular buildings.

agreed frontier along the Watling Street, dividing the Danelaw on one side from English England on the other. His descendants then went on to win back all of England and to unite it for the first time as one kingdom. Linguistic evidence suggests there was considerable Scandinavian settlement in northeastern England and to a lesser extent in East Anglia. In fact, even the historical basis for all of this is not entirely uncomplicated, and the numbers of settlers have been hotly disputed even where there are many Scandinavian place names. The archaeological evidence is even less straightforward.

In the first place, the revisionist view of the Vikings as peaceful characters has not always won support. In the Orkneys Anna Ritchie has argued for integration between the native Picts and the incoming Scandinavians. She excavated a settlement at Buckquoy, near the tidal island of Birsay off the Orkney Mainland, where native houses, stone-walled buildings of an oval or figure-of-eight shape, were succeeded by rectangular Norse houses. The objects found in both types of building, and the way of life of their inhabitants, did not, however, seem to have changed much, if at all. On the island of Birsay itself there are both Norse houses and signs of earlier Pictish occupation, but the relationship between the two is not very clear. Of the Picts on Birsay nothing now remains except a replica of a

RIGHT *Carving of three Pictish warriors from Birsay, Orkney.*

this is most peculiar, and not all the details will be clear until excavation has been completed in a year or two. It was initially thought that the bones might be the result of a defeat or massacre of the Mercian army, and that after the bodies had been left elsewhere for a while, perhaps on the battlefield, they had been brought back for burial in this ancient Mercian burial place. But the mound and the crouched burials look far more like Vikings than Christian Saxons. So had the Vikings buried their enemies?

That was what Martin Biddle thought when we filmed him. But later examination of the bones seems to show that they had not suffered greatly from sword cuts. An alternative explanation then is that here we have a Viking chief (the giant) who was laid out with many of his followers. Since the skeletons do not show signs of sword wounds, and it is hard to believe so many adult males would have been sacrificed, even to attend an important leader to Valhalla, it seems more likely that they died of disease, possibly a plague. Or of boredom from being cooped up in a fort all winter with nothing to do but mend the ship. It is just possible that this massacre also will turn out, like Harling, to have been just something to do with medieval graveyard clearance after all, but that would not explain the mound or the crouched burials dug through it. It is a most fascinating site, even if it does remain to be seen whether it provides direct evidence for Viking slaughter or for burial – either would be a sorely needed archaeological demonstration of their presence in Britain.

Other Viking burials are surprisingly few and far between, especially on mainland England. More have been found in the northern islands and several have been excavated on the Isle of Man. One of these burials was in a ship under a mound which seemed to have been put deliberately on top of earlier native Christian graves. In another there was a female skeleton with a large hole in her skull as well as the main male burial. Recently another female burial has been found on Man. In Ireland again few burials are known, apart from the cemetery at Kilmainham near Dublin. In England only three possible cemeteries have been found. These are at Repton, described above, at Ingleby which is not far from Repton, and another group of burials under Kildale church in Yorkshire. Otherwise all that we have are occasional scattered instances of burials with Viking objects. Perhaps burials with Saxon objects of ninth- or tenth-century date should be included as well, since it was not normal practice for Saxons to bury grave-goods with their dead at that time.

The linguistic and historical evidence for large-scale Scandinavian settlement in northern and eastern England might be minimized, the suggested numbers might be reduced – but it really cannot be altogether ignored. Yet the archaeological evidence of the kind one would expect before suggesting a prehistoric invasion simply does not exist in sufficient quantity.

The answer may lie in a process which has parallels in what had happened amongst the Saxons themselves a few centuries previously. The pagan burials which were the sign of the arrival of these barbarians, as we have seen in the last chapter, gave way to graves without objects after conversion to Christianity. Perhaps the same thing happened to the Vikings, and they also became Christian and ceased to have distinctive burials. This would suggest that a great many of the Christian Saxons had survived to convert them, and that they thought it worth bothering to turn to a religion which to begin with might not have looked as if it was serving its devotees very well. The conversion Alfred forced on the Danish leader Guthrum and his followers must have been reasonably effective for burial customs to have changed so completely. It is also worth noticing that we have two changes of burial rite which appear to suggest rather different things: on the one hand, in the seventh century the pagan Saxons became Christian and ceased to bury grave-goods. In other words, there was a change in burial rite within an existing population. On the other, we have incomers taking over the native burial rite and becoming archaeologically indistinguishable from the local people. Both changes show clearly that we cannot make simple equations between changes in burial practice or styles of pottery and changes in the populations concerned.

Information from other sources is no more helpful. Isolated pieces of Scandinavian metalwork could as well have arrived in Britain through trade as in the luggage of invaders, though some of the Irish and British objects found in Scandinavian graves do look as if they have been looted – for example, broken pieces of book mounts that have been made into parts of necklaces.

One area where people do talk confidently is in relation to 'Norse' houses, rectangular buildings with central hearths and wide benches running down the long sides. But here again interpretation may not be so simple. The difficulty is that we don't always know enough about what the local native houses looked like to be able to say when we have a new type. In Orkney and on the Hebrides one can see a change, but in England some kind of rectangular timber house was

LEFT *Picture stone from Gotland in Sweden, showing scenes probably from Norse mythology, including representations of a boat and a larger ship.*

RIGHT *Stone carved with a runic inscription from Sweden. The letters are formed from straight lines, suitable for cutting in wood, and they are arranged in a long narrow frame which on this stone takes the form of two snake-like beasts.*

they probably contain the names of people who had managed to seize the throne, and who legitimated their claim by a little judicious doctoring of their genealogy to fit it into the appropriate royal family tree.

Sometimes these kings fought each other, or their relations: there is no reason to suppose their home life was any more pleasant than that of the Frankish kings, portrayed by Gregory of Tours, which included fratricidal quarrels and murders by one member of a family of the others, not stopping short of grandmothers. Anglo-Saxons fought Britons and both fought each other and some kingdoms began to expand at the expense of others. By the time Bede wrote his history, in the early eighth century, the main Anglo-Saxon kingdoms were Kent, Sussex, Wessex, Essex, East Anglia, Mercia and Northumbria.

Under the vigorous King Offa, who ruled from 757 to 796, Mercia became very large, taking over East Anglia and Kent, and threatening Wessex. As early as a century later Bishop Asser, biographer of King Alfred, recorded that Offa had built a great dyke along the frontier between Mercia and Wales, from sea to sea. Although a bit ravaged by hikers' feet, the standing sections of bank and ditch are still impressive and even today seem a significant barrier, particularly as the ditch is full of nettles. Much of Offa's Dyke has been worn down over the centuries, but David Hill from Manchester has managed to trace the missing stretches and has cut more than a hundred sections through it.

Other linear earthworks were built around the same time – including the Danevirke in Denmark and also perhaps a series of banks and ditches in East Anglia near Cambridge, which lie across the Icknield Way. These East Anglian defences have been interpreted as belonging to a period when the Britons were defending themselves against invading Anglo-Saxons. In fact they are just as likely to have been put up later by the East Anglians trying to defend themselves against attack from the south or west, perhaps indeed from King Offa. It is however difficult to prove this. A section cut some years ago through the largest, the Devil's Dyke on Newmarket Heath, failed to narrow the dates beyond what was known already, that it must have been built after the end of central Roman control, and before the late Saxon period.

Apart from his expansionist achievements, King Offa was important for the economy of England. He issued coinage on a larger scale than his predecessors, though he took over some of their

Coin of King Offa, showing his bust and name.

moneyers. The silver penny which he used was to remain the standard unit of English currency for many centuries, until long after the Norman Conquest. Many of those coins have been found abroad, evidence of the increasing volume of trade with the Continent. The reign of Offa in England was partly contemporary with that of the Emperor Charlemagne, who ruled a territory larger than had been seen in Europe since the days of the Roman Empire, which Charlemagne was of course trying to emulate. This great ruler found time to write to Offa about such matters as the length of cloaks exported from England, the type of black stones to be sent from the Continent, and the protection of traders in both countries.

The trade the rulers were discussing passed through ports on the North Sea coast, such as Quentovic in northern France, a site now lost, or Dorestad, near modern Utrecht in the Netherlands, or Ribe and Hedeby in Denmark. In England London and York have for a long time been historically attested as important trading ports in the eighth century, but archaeological evidence for this period has been elusive until very recently. It now appears that we were looking for it in the wrong place in both cities. The Roman walled circuits which later became the nuclei for the medieval cities of York and London were not where the merchants that Bede records were carrying out their trade.

In London two scholars, Martin Biddle and Alan Vince, realized simultaneously that not only is 'Aldwych' an interesting name, since 'wich' appears to have some connotation of town or port, but also that most of the middle Saxon objects found in London have come from that area. This is one of those ideas which looks obvious once someone has had the sense to think of it, and it seems to have been confirmed by excavations during 1985. So in the days of King Offa ships were tying up along the Strand, outside the walled city of London. Similarly in York, an excavation in the autumn of 1985 outside the walls, at an old glass works near the confluence of the rivers Ouse and Foss, has turned up more eighth-century material in a few weeks than has been found in the whole of the city during two hundred years of excavation. In the next year or two our knowledge of eighth-century London and York may at last come to rival that of other towns, such as Southampton and Ipswich. We may then be able to see whether they were already pre-eminent then, as they were to become later.

Meanwhile, we do know quite a lot about Southampton and Ipswich. At Southampton the eighth-century town lay to the east of

Offa's Dyke. This surviving stretch of bank and ditch snakes across country, marking out the Anglo-Saxon frontier between England and Wales.

597. The detail of the conversion of ordinary people, as opposed to that of kings and nobles, is also not easy to establish from Bede. Either people followed their leaders very docilely into the new religion, or they in fact remained very far from true believers whatever their nominal faith. Or in fact part of the population was still British and was also still Christian. This last is not an idea Bede allows for and it must be confessed that there is at present little evidence for it, but I think it should not be ruled out as a possibility.

In outline it is clear that during the seventh century all of England became officially Christian, whatever odd pagan practices might survive amongst ordinary people. This conversion can be seen in changes in the archaeological record, which, if we had met them in a prehistoric context, would have been seen as proof of an invasion. If a small group of monks constitutes an invasion then that was what it was, but I don't think most of us would describe it in that way. It is true that there may have been a political element in the conversion, in that Ethelbert of Kent had married a Christian Frankish wife, Bertha, and he may have been to some extent in a subordinate relationship to the Frankish king, who may have had something to do with the Christian mission. But of that Bede does not tell us, preferring the inspiration of Pope Gregory at the sight of angelic Angles in the slave market.

Conversion to Christianity was marked by a change in burial ritual, new styles in art, the appearance of types of object not seen before, and the reappearance of stone architecture. Burials gradually changed from the accompanied pagan cremations or inhumations to the normal Christian burial without grave-goods (apart from some notable exceptions, such as St Cuthbert, and probably many royal and aristocratic graves, which did still have rich assemblages of objects). This is most frustrating for archaeologists since the main source of datable metalwork thus disappears. Such jewellery as we do find, in the latest accompanied graves and in occasional stray finds, shows how Continental styles, ultimately deriving from Byzantium, replaced many of the old Germanic brooch types. There are more delicate necklaces with pendants, and cloaks fastened by pins attached to fine chains. There are specifically Christian artefacts, such as cross-shaped pendants or chalices.

And there are manuscripts. The illuminated manuscripts produced in Britain and Ireland during the late seventh and eighth centuries are extraordinary creations: all the skills which had gone into creating a piece of convoluted animal ornament on something

FAR RIGHT *A carpet page from the* Lindisfarne Gospels, *written and illuminated in Northumbria towards the end of the seventh century.*

like the gold buckle from Sutton Hoo were redeployed in the creation of manuscripts. Actual gold- and enamel-working techniques would have been needed for making the fittings for the covers of the books, and the leather was probably also ornamented. But within, there are whole pages of ornament, the carpet pages. If you look closely at a carpet page from, for example, the most famous of these manuscripts, the *Lindisfarne Gospels*, it can be seen that the overall pattern is made up from many tiny intertwined animals.

In fact, the manuscripts represent a remarkable fusion of three different styles: Celtic, Germanic and classical. The human figures of the evangelists, and the whole idea of the gospels and of the written word, is of Mediterranean inspiration. The details of many of the ornaments, on the other hand, are either Germanic beasts or Celtic spirals. Similarly, sculptured stone crosses are Christian in inspiration, and they carry ornament of vine-scrolls which is clearly Mediterranean. But the vines often have animals sitting in their branches.

The churches of this period may have been built of timber, much like ordinary houses: traces of post-holes under later churches are all that remains of these, except for one building at Yeavering which has been interpreted as a church. Anglo-Saxons who had travelled, like the Northumbrians, Benedict Biscop and St Wilfrid, knew that proper churches were built in stone, and they used stone themselves even if it meant bringing the masons from France. A handful of stone churches dating back to this period remains, most in Canterbury or in Northumbria, though it is often difficult to be sure which bits of the buildings can really claim such an early date.

Eighth-century England was different in various ways from sixth-century England. The changes suggest, rightly, closer contact with the Continent and developments in the organization of society, but they happened without a major influx of foreigners. England had become a prosperous country, with towns, literature and liturgy, churches and palaces, kings and bishops. If we go from this period, before the Viking raids, to the tenth century, after the worst of them, what differences emerge? In the first place, this jump is itself a sign of disruption, because it is actually not easy to date many things precisely to the ninth century, which was clearly a time when much was destroyed and lost. A crisis can be inferred precisely because it is so difficult to bridge the gap between the two phases. Secondly, many of the observable differences are explicable in terms of a pressing need for defence. Instead of the large undefended sprawling trading centres, like Southampton and probably London and York, which existed in the eighth century, there are smaller defended towns in the tenth.

A whole network of these defended towns grew up over the south of England and was then extended northwards. These are the 'burhs', many of which were built by King Alfred and his descendants. In some cases old Roman walls were used, as at Winchester, while other towns were laid out for the first time, in neat rectangular patterns, like Wallingford. The banks and ditches of a few can still be seen, notably at Wareham near Poole in Dorset, where the whole circuit can still be walked. It was not only in England that townspeople retreated behind their walls: Birka and Hedeby got their ramparts at this time, and other places, like Dorestad, which did not, seem to have been destroyed and disappeared. Southampton came to an end on its eighth-century site, and it was probably then that the walled circuits of York and London became once more the focus of the towns. Tenth-century towns were forts, where eighth-century towns had been undefended market places.

By the later tenth century England was a single political unit. From the time when Alfred burnt the cakes in despairing refuge in Athelney, it took him and his descendants a century to conquer and unite England. In 973 Edgar, Alfred's grandson, was crowned in Bath and received the submission of even Welsh and Scottish kings. We know this from historical sources, but they are consistent with the archaeological evidence. The burhs do look like parts of a logical system of defence and administration for the whole country. The same coinage was used throughout the country and it is of a good and standard quality, regularly recalled and reminted despite the fact that mints existed in so many places, in most of the burhs. There was better quality pottery, wheel-thrown and hard-fired, distributed from several sites in England over much of the eastern part of the country. Many more churches were built and there was a renewal of art associated with the Church.

The country might have become a unity, politically, simply as the result of a strong dynasty. If Offa had had an equally vigorous son and grandson, Mercia might have swallowed up the whole of England rather earlier than Wessex actually did so. The idea of fortifying towns may in fact have begun in Mercia: the defences at some Mercian towns, like Hereford and Tamworth, just might predate the Alfredian burhs. The coinage had already been reorganized in the time of Offa. Taken alone, the English evidence might be interpreted simply as a demonstration of the strength of the West Saxon dynasty in the tenth century, and of its achievement in uniting what had been several separate small kingdoms and creating one strong centralized state. Put in the context of the rest of northern Europe the Viking threat becomes much clearer.

All those towns did not disappear or build great ramparts for nothing. Many coins have been found in Scandinavia, especially from England, an imbalance which normal trading activity would not have achieved. And although there are not as many signs of Scandinavian presence as one might expect, they are still there. In Scandinavia itself there are direct and indirect traces of the raids. There are the looted objects and coins, the great hoards of silver brought back from east and west. There are also the fortified towns, signs that raiding was not confined to foreign countries. The arrival of Christianity in Scandinavia and the appearance of Christian burials and churches could of course be the result of a combination of foreign contacts and peaceful missions, like those which had converted other Germanic peoples.

The development of larger political units, especially the formation of Denmark, might also have occurred anyway, and may have been as much a cause as a result of Viking raids, but it is interesting that a stronger political unit should have appeared in Denmark as well as England. Even if one does not take all of Harold Bluetooth's claims on the Jellinge stone at face value, he does seem to have had a notable effect on the landscape. It was probably he who built the strange round forts, Aggersborg and Fyrkat on Jutland, Trelleborg on Seeland and Nonnebakken under modern Odense. These were all built to the same strict geometrical plan, with crossing streets and bow-sided houses laid out in squares. The siting of some of these forts shows little regard for topography and the absolute rigidity of the plans suggests a degree of megalomania in their builder.

These forts were once interpreted as barracks for troops invading Britain under Harold's son, Svein Forkbeard, but the dates are wrong and also the position of the forts doesn't look very sensible for an attack on England to the west, since they are if anything easterly. It is more likely that they are to do with imposing and maintaining internal control. Other major engineering works may have belonged to the same period, such as a long causeway at Ravning Enge. On the other hand, a canal through the island of Samsø is probably earlier,

Aerial view of the Viking fort at Trelleborg in Denmark, with the foundations of large bow-sided houses shown laid out in regular blocks.

as is the Danevirke, so there was already a tradition of large-scale engineering in Denmark before the tenth century.

It is interesting to speculate whether the English and Danish states would have developed anyway, without the stimulus of the need to organize, whether for attack or defence. Taken altogether, however, the nature of the archaeological evidence for the North Sea region from the eighth to the tenth centuries does show that it was a time of great insecurity, and that the threat came from Scandinavia, and was directed against the relatively peaceful and wealthy lands of Britain and the Carolingian empire. The Viking raids would, I think, emerge even without historical records, but it would perhaps be less clear whether there was any kind of substantial settlement of Scandinavians. And it is still arguable that this lack of much direct evidence for settlement reflects the fact that there was not very much, although I suspect that the weight of historical and linguistic material does point to a noticeable influx in some areas. If this is so, the Viking settlement has, exasperatingly, not left us with the kinds of evidence one might have expected.

The Northmen in their next incarnation, as Normans, had a more immediately drastic effect on the country they invaded.

Chapter 7 | **1066 and All That**

The Norman Conquest is the last and best-known successful invasion of England, 1066 the most memorable date in English history. The story has been told very often, perhaps best and most vividly in one of the earliest accounts, on the Bayeux Tapestry, still kept in Bayeux (where it is known as the tapestry of Queen Matilda). To film it we had to get up very early, as at Stonehenge, which is not easy if the previous evening has been spent enjoying French food and wine. The tapestry used to be hung round the walls of a room, but has now been redisplayed around a large central case. This is probably better from the point of view of preservation, but it removes any illusion that it is still hanging on the walls of a hall, as it was intended to. It is not really a tapestry but an embroidery, one of the few surviving examples of the embroidery for which Anglo-Saxon women were famous, since, although it is said to have been made for Bishop Odo of Bayeux, William the Conqueror's half-brother, it was made by English ladies. In some ways it reflects that dual origin: in outline it is propaganda for William, showing how he was the rightful and legitimate King of England, but it can also be read as an epic tragedy, the story of the downfall of Harold after he broke the oath William had extracted from him. It is also a good comic strip, with a commentary in Latin – miraculously translated via headphones to Japanese, German, or Swedish at need.

So here was an incontrovertible military invasion by an efficient army under a very tough leader, who had been fighting to maintain his position in his homeland and then to strengthen it as long as he had been able to hold weapons. In the years after 1066 there was a clean sweep of the upper echelons of British society: the leading Anglo-Saxons were dead or in exile and both the lay aristocracy and the upper levels of the Church saw a considerable change of

discussing the most dramatic contributions of the Normans to the landscape, castles and Romanesque architecture.

Castles were not invented by the Norman dukes. The idea of a fortified residence goes back a long way, and the dividing line between a communal fort, like a hillfort, designed to protect the whole community, and a private defended house or castle, is not always at all easy to define. Were brochs the first castles? Were hillforts really all so communal – or were some chiefs holed up there against their revolting peasants as well as their neighbours? There does at least seem to be a clear difference between walled towns, like those of Roman Britain or Anglo-Saxon England, and private castles. The kind of society which devotes effort to creating a system of defence for all the population, with an overall plan developed by a central authority even if carried out by locals, is not the same as one where powerful individuals are able to surround themselves with walls and barricades, as much to terrify and subjugate the local population as to protect the inmates. The appearance of the latter is the clearest archaeological sign of the Norman Conquest.

Much scholarly ink has been spilt over the origin of the castle in Europe, with the debate often fuelled as much by disagreement over the definition of terms as by hard facts. At all events, there are certainly castles outside Normandy which were built as early as the tenth century. One of the best preserved is at Langeais in Anjou, built by the wicked Count Fulk the Black, alleged descendant of the devil and ancestor of the occasionally devilish Henry II and his brood of quarrelsome sons. The ruin of Fulk's castle lies in the grounds of a much later château famous for its tapestries. A massive stone wall stands on a large mound, pierced high up by small round-headed windows. The Norman ducal residences at Fécamp and Caen had stone walls around them and could also be seen as castles of a sort, though they are usually differentiated as fortified palaces.

Romanesque architecture is also not a Norman invention, but a style that was widespread throughout Europe. As its name suggests, it is descended from Roman architecture, much of which must still have been standing as models for medieval builders. The windows at Langeais, with their brick arches, are a simple version of the most characteristic Romanesque feature, the round-headed arch. Carolingian and Anglo-Saxon buildings could be described as belonging to the early stage of Romanesque architecture, but the name is usually associated in people's minds with the great buildings of the Church, like the abbeys William and his wife Matilda built at

Caen, or Durham Cathedral in England. The Normans did not invent Romanesque architecture any more than they invented castles, and both phenomena can be found throughout Europe and even, arguably, in England, before 1066. But the scale on which they built, the sheer number of their castles and the size and magnificence of the churches, is new. The impact the Normans had on England derives from their organization, their efficiency, and from the wealth they had at their disposal once they had conquered England.

Like the Vikings before them, the Normans were attracted by the wealth of England and this was at least part of the inspiration for the Conquest. Late Anglo-Saxon England was not a poor backward country: it was far wealthier and more civilized than Normandy. In fact the Normans rather despised the English for their culture, regarding them as effete and long-haired (even in 1066 the military mind preferred 'short-back-and-sides' haircuts!). England was famous for its embroideries and gold work, of which only a few tiny fragments remain today.

From written accounts it is possible to piece together an impression of the lavishness of the metalwork, textiles, sculpture and manuscripts to be found in churches and monasteries, and probably

Late Saxon silver disc brooches with elaborate animal ornament. They were dug up several years ago by a grave-digger at Pentney in Norfolk.

in aristocratic homes as well. Anglo-Saxons seem to have preferred to work on a small scale, producing delicate ivories and fragile gold embroidery. Their churches tended to be rather small, with complicated additions in the form of towers and twisting staircases, crypts and elaborate west fronts. Buildings were often changed by accretion, with the older parts incorporated in the new rather than the whole thing being knocked down and built afresh. The complicated plans which might result are well shown by Martin and Birthe Biddle's excavations of the Old Minster at Winchester. Here, lots of added towers and chapels make the plan look as much as anything like a child's drawing of a space rocket.

Such churches would have been elaborately decorated, with painted wall plaster, stained glass, gilded statues and elaborate wall hangings. Today these can only be pieced together from remnants. The pieces of metal or ivory which we prize today as masterpieces of Anglo-Saxon art would probably have seemed insignificant to a contemporary: in fact their taste might have been a bit too flashy for some of us, with all that paint and gilding.

There have been many times of upheaval and disaster since the days of the Anglo-Saxons, when some of what they produced was destroyed, including the dissolution of the monasteries, the Civil War and two World Wars. Yet it was at the time of the Norman Conquest that many of the products of Anglo Saxon culture went forever. The invaders took away literally cartloads of treasure, ransacked for their family homes back in Normandy (the next generation, which lived in England, may have brought some back, if it had not been melted down altogether). Some accounts of the Conquest present it as a 'Good Thing', bringing England back into contact with Europe and so into the mainstream of European culture. This view ignores the fact that there had always been contact across the Channel, both economic and cultural, and that the traffic had gone both ways. Charlemagne had turned to English monasteries when he needed scholars, while in later centuries refugees of various kinds went from England to the Continent, and sometimes came back again – like St Dunstan, or King Edward the Confessor. It is probably more likely that the development of native English culture was set back for generations.

One effect of the Conquest was, then, clearly destructive. But perhaps we should begin by assessing what might be seen as a positive result, the construction of large stone buildings, notably castles and churches.

FAR RIGHT *Illuminated page from the* Benedictional of St Aethelwold, *Bishop of Winchester and Abbot of Abingdon in the tenth century. This is an especially rich manuscript, illuminated in gold as well as with paint.*

As we have seen, castles are not peculiarly Norman. Even in England there has been hot debate as to whether any existed before 1066. Historical sources suggest a few were built in the reign of Edward the Confessor, but these are sometimes discounted on the grounds that Edward was almost a Norman himself, with a Norman mother, who had lived many years in exile in Normandy. Somehow anything that he did is counted as a trial run for William. However, there is a little archaeological evidence to suggest that at least some Anglo-Saxon, or Anglo-Danish, thegns were protecting their homes with earthen banks and ditches. At Sulgrave in Northamptonshire a late Saxon manor house preceded a Norman manor which had a defensive ringwork, but it is not entirely clear how substantial any pre-Conquest defences were. At Goltho in Lincolnshire successive phases of the manor house, from Saxon to Norman, show an evolution of the defences which begins before 1066. The late Saxon buildings within the old Roman fort at Portchester in Hampshire have been interpreted as the residence of a thegn, partly because of a structure which might have been a tower. Portchester became a Norman castle, and perhaps it had already provided some of the same defensive functions earlier.

Finding a few pre-Conquest fortified houses – and there may be many more as yet unidentified – still does not alter the fact that only after 1066 was the whole countryside dotted with castles. Most of these were initially of the simple motte-and-bailey variety, known to many of us from primary school model-building days. The motte is the mound, now usually covered with grass, which had a tower on top of it, the keep. At first, most towers were built of timber and only later replaced in stone. Some of the mottes seem to have contained timber frameworks, foundations for the towers, and it is not always clear whether the tower was built first with the mound heaped up around its lower stages. It would have been quicker and safer to do this than to build the tower on top of the mound. The bailey is the defended courtyard below and beside the motte. This is the classic, simple kind of castle which was put up in its hundreds by the new lords to control their conquered lands, presumably using the forced labour of the Saxon peasants. Other lords, as at Goltho and Sulgrave, built or rebuilt ringworks, circular banked and ditched enclosures with a hall and other buildings inside.

At Hen Domen, near Montgomery on the Welsh border, there is a classic motte-and-bailey castle which Philip Barker has been excavating now for many years, applying the same meticulous techniques as at Wroxeter. Here, too, disentangling the traces of timber structures has rather altered our thinking about this type of site. Hen Domen, whose name means 'Old Mound' in Welsh, was probably the first Montgomery castle, built by Roger of Montgomery, one of William's henchmen, in the years after the Conquest. In 1102 it passed to the de Boulers family – one of whom had the good fortune to marry a lady called Hillaria Trussebut. The castle controlled an important crossing over the River Severn, a point on a major route from England to Wales where the Romans had built a fort long before. In the thirteenth century a new castle was built some miles away, on top of a rocky hill above what is now Montgomery town. From this later castle there is a view across into Wales beyond Offa's Dyke, but from the top of a timber tower on Hen Domen there would have been a good view of the river-crossing and it may have been kept on a while as an outpost.

Reconstructions of the baileys of medieval castles often show them rather as they appear today, as pleasant green spaces with a few tidy buildings scattered about. Philip Barker has shown it was not like that at Hen Domen. Within what is really not a very large space (and he has only dug a quarter of it), there are the remains of dozens of buildings. Not all the buildings would have been in use at the same time, but there would have been quite enough of them to have created a most claustrophobic huddle within the defences, especially if a palisade had been added to the bank. Most of the time anyone inside would not have been able to see out and it could have felt like being in prison. Castles had to be partly self-sufficient and so space had to be found not only for living quarters for the lord, his family and servants, the garrison and hangers-on, but also for animals and food stores, and workshops such as a smithy, a bakery and a brewhouse. All of this must have made for a crowded and unpleasant place, even when not under siege.

The small finds of pottery and metal from Hen Domen are surprisingly few and uninspiring. Romantic pictures of life in a castle, with minstrels and troubadours, do not fit the remains from this small tough border outpost. There is little to show that this was a medieval castle rather than some hitherto unidentified kind of Iron Age fort, except for the type of potsherd found there and some carbon-14 dates, together with the historical record. Life at Hen Domen was probably not much different in the twelfth century from life lived in local forts in the centuries before Christ: it was certainly far less pleasant than the life of the citizens of Roman Wroxeter.

OVERLEAF *Aerial view of Hen Domen Castle, Powys, showing pre-Norman ridged fields surrounding the castle.*

221

FAR RIGHT *The keep of Castle Hedingham in Essex. The windows in the lower storey are very small but in the upper floors, where the need for security was less immediate, they are larger, especially at the top where the lord and his family had their quarters.*

As soon as they could afford it, the wealthier lords replaced timber towers with stone. Castle Hedingham in Essex was built by Aubrey de Vere around 1140, using stone brought from Barnack in Northamptonshire. The massive keep still stands on its mound, despite having been taken twice by siege during the reign of King John. Inside, successive floors can be reached by spiral staircases, the windows getting larger as you go up. There are fine decorated door and window arches, and the second-floor main hall is spanned by what is said to be 'the largest Norman arch in Europe'. The garrison would have lived below the hall, while the family and the ladies would have occupied the top floor. The idea was that the top was the safest place, the last refuge, though anyone sheltering there would have been trapped if a successful enemy were to set fire to the place.

Castle Rising in Norfolk was built around the same time as Hedingham, but it looks more like a defended hall than a tower keep and it sits within a ringwork rather than on top of a motte. Another Norfolk castle, Castle Acre, has been excavated and shown to have had a very complicated history. Like Castle Rising, it began as a strong stone-built hall, at least two storeys high. This was probably built before 1085 when Gundrada, wife of the owner, William de Warenne, died there in childbirth. Later the hall was converted into a keep, rather smaller in ground area than the hall, but much taller. The earthwork defences were modified and strengthened several times, and the ground level of the keep was raised by packing the original ground floor of the hall with chalk. Since excavation, this castle has looked more like an urban building site than a rural ruin, and the scaffolding still there recently gave it the air of a still-besieged fort. Let us hope some not too drastic method of displaying it safely will soon be found – there are difficulties because it was built of a stone which is not very easily consolidated, and the walls are in danger of crumbling away if permanently exposed to the weather.

The king himself built in stone from the start. The White Tower in London and Colchester Castle, the latter built on the foundations of a Roman temple, were designed as fortified palaces, like the ducal residences in Normandy. Life within was presumably more comfortable than it was at Hen Domen.

Castle building was changed and adapted throughout the Middle Ages in response to political situations and military technology. Every development in siege warfare was countered by changes in castle design until eventually artillery rendered them obsolete. If the

of the stone they are built of, pale Barnack limestone. Because of this they seem closer to the churches in Normandy that were built of Caen stone – which was also shipped to England for some buildings.

Two major examples of the Norman use of this stone are in Caen itself, the churches built by William and his wife Matilda in expiation for their uncanonical marriage within the forbidden degrees of kinship. The Abbaye aux Dames, built by Matilda, was begun in 1062, but William's Abbaye aux Hommes is post-Conquest. (William was buried there, but the tomb has been pillaged more than once and now only a femur survives – this was recently examined and shown to have belonged to an adult male, so maybe this really is all we have left of William the Conqueror.) Other Norman churches, for example at Bayeux, Rouen and on top of the rock on Mont St Michel, can be compared with the English series. There is something very similar in the massive simplicity of all these churches, with their tall round pillars, round arches, aisles below triforia and clerestoreys. Some connection between Normandy and England would be inescapably suggested even if there were no historical records.

Some of the smaller churches were partly or entirely rebuilt as well as many new ones being founded. Good examples are the church at Melbourne in Derbyshire, and part of Christchurch Priory in Dorset, while Iffley in Oxfordshire has an elaborate Norman west front. Doorways often survive when the rest has gone, although sometimes not in their original position. There are also fonts with Romanesque sculpture, like the one from Castle Frome in Hereford and Worcester. In the same county is Kilpeck, whose elaborate doorway has men and beasts entwined in a way more than a little reminiscent of Viking sculpture.

It is still worth asking how purely 'Norman' this whole outburst of building was. The similarities between the two sides of the Channel are obvious. But does the physical evidence alone demonstrate that these similarities were brought about by a violent conquest of one side by the other? After all, some Romanesque architecture was built before 1066. Edward the Confessor built Westminster Abbey, which was completed in time for his own funeral. Although it was largely pulled down in the thirteenth century, to be replaced by the present tourist attraction, we have some idea of its appearance from the Bayeux tapestry. It seems to have looked very like Jumièges, begun in 1037, which Edward might have seen during his exile. If royal patronage had made the style

LEFT *Stone font from St Michael's Church, Castle Frome, Hereford and Worcester. Carved around 1140, this is one of a group of fine carvings of this date from this part of the country.*

FAR RIGHT *The abbey church of Notre Dame, Jumièges, Normandy, built before the Norman Conquest of England.*

popular, the Romanesque might have spread through England in a purely peaceful context. On the architectural evidence alone one could argue for a redirection of resources on a large scale to church building from the later eleventh century, and perhaps for the arrival of some architects from Normandy. A dramatic increase in church building and rebuilding had happened before, in the tenth century, with the renewal of religious fervour and of ecclesiastical finances after the Viking raids. A military invasion might not seem at all the best context for such a religious revival.

But Norman building was marked not only by the scale of the resources involved but also by a total disregard for ancient Anglo-Saxon churches, saints' burial places and royal tombs, marking out this phase of church building as a break with tradition. Without the Conquest there surely would have been more large Romanesque buildings like Westminster, and the style would have percolated down eventually. But there would not have been so many new buildings and there would have been more attempts to retain the old fabric within the new, even in the larger ones. The old attention to detail, to paintings, statues and ornaments, would not have given way so quickly to massive simplicity and austerity.

The castles and cathedrals of twelfth-century England would alone suggest a picture of sudden and violent reorganization. That might just have happened for internal reasons, because of the emergence of a new and militaristic dynasty or simply of a vigorous heir to an existing royal line. Twelfth-century England, like tenth-century England, might be interpreted as the creation of a strong native ruler who had rearranged his kingdom himself. But that would be difficult to reconcile with the way castles were clearly planted to suppress the local population and not as defences against an incoming enemy. Exactly when one might have put the Conquest on archaeological grounds is not easy to say: the Romanesque buildings and castles of the reign of Edward the Confessor might suggest a few decades before 1066, whilst the date of the majority of castles and cathedrals would take it into the twelfth century. We cannot rid ourselves of the knowledge that the Norman Conquest did take place, but in so far as that is possible it does seem that, even without the historical accounts, the archaeological evidence would suggest a military invasion, possibly from Normandy, some time after the middle of the eleventh century.

Castles and cathedrals are only half the story, and we still need to see what the archaeological evidence tells us about the fate of

Winchester is not a model for most of the parish churches of England. It is only in recent years, following the patient work of Harold Taylor in cataloguing surviving Anglo-Saxon churches, that it has become clear how many of these there are. In 1978, 267 churches could be listed, identified from structural analysis and visible architectural detail as at least partly Anglo-Saxon. As we shall see, more should probably be added to that number.

Little remains of the earliest churches, since these were mostly built of timber and have survived only as post-holes under later excavated churches, such as Wharram Percy or Barton-on-Humber. The timber church which does still remain at Greensted in Essex cannot be taken as a model for these early churches, as it seems to represent later Scandinavian influence. The split oak tree-trunks which form the walls now rest on a Victorian brick plinth, and dormer windows in the roof give it a rather cosy cottage-like appearance.

A few stone churches can be dated to the seventh or eighth centuries, usually from historical sources. Most of these are in Kent, where the first mission was based, such as St Pancras and St Martin's at Canterbury. There is also a group in northern England, including Jarrow, where a foundation stone gives the precise date of 23 April 684 (or 685) for the dedication of St Paul's. Unfortunately, most of that church was demolished in 1782 and what we have now is even later than that, a creation of Gilbert Scott in the nineteenth century (except, that is, for the chancel, which is Anglo-Saxon).

A better idea of an early Saxon church is given by Escomb in County Durham. This simple two-celled building still sits in its round churchyard, now in the middle of a housing estate. It was at one time larger, with a western annexe and a side chapel to the north of the nave, but its present classic simplicity makes it a model for the reconstruction of early Saxon churches. The proportions of the nave and chancel arch, which are tall and narrow, are a classic feature of Anglo-Saxon architecture, as are the massive stones (the 'megalithic quoins') which form the corners of the nave and the sides of the chancel arch. The arch itself may have been transported complete from the nearby Roman fort at Binchester, a likely source also for the rest of the stone used. Roman sites were often used as quarries by later builders. The windows are small, with intentionally splayed openings designed to reflect as much light as possible from the small space. Their size is probably for economy in the use of glass – or even, if they were left unglazed, an attempt to cut down the draught.

Amongst possibly surviving early churches, that at Brixworth in Northamptonshire is now the most impressive. There is dispute as to its exact date, and much of its present appearance is owed to Charles Watkins, who was Vicar of Brixworth for forty years in the last century. He removed many later accretions and created something which probably does look like the Saxon church, apart from the aisles or side chapels which once existed. The arches of these aisles still exist, but they are blocked up. Both these aisles and the doors and windows of the early phases have arches made from bricks which have been assumed to be Roman. Recent analysis appears to confirm this date for some of them, but others seem later. Brixworth is currently the subject of a major research project which it is hoped will resolve some of the problems involved in working out

The Anglo-Saxon church at Escomb, County Durham. The two small round-headed windows are original; the others are later insertions.

its dating and development. One interesting result that has emerged so far has come from a careful plotting of all the different kinds of stone used in the construction of the church. This shows how the source of materials changed from one building stage to the next.

The majority of churches defined as Anglo-Saxon belong to a later period than Escomb or Brixworth, to the tenth or early eleventh centuries, when there was much rebuilding after the Viking destruction. However, some of these churches do seem to have complex histories and parts of even the 'late' churches may belong to an earlier date. Features of later churches, apart from those already listed in connection with Escomb, include narrow applied strips of stone, called pilaster strips, which can be seen on two well-preserved towers at Earls Barton and Barton-on-Humber. These seem to be purely decorative features, which have sometimes been explained as stone versions of familiar half-timbering. Some details can be traced to contemporary architecture on the Continent, though stylistic arguments are often complicated by the sparsity of evidence on both sides of the Channel.

A number of churches have been extensively examined in recent years, with the walls recorded in very great detail. This often reveals unexpected information about alterations and rebuilding, to add to that recovered from excavation. At Deerhurst in Gloucester, for example, there was once an apsidal end to the chancel, now demolished, and it is clear that several phases of building took place before 1066. At Barton-on-Humber a very small church was built originally, with the tower forming the nave sandwiched between a small chancel and a baptistery. Over the centuries the original building was gradually altered and grew. Warwick Rodwell was able to trace this growth because this is a redundant church and he could excavate the whole of the interior, not something that congregations of churches still in use usually welcome. He also excavated part of the cemetery, and found Anglo-Saxon burials still in wooden coffins. We have already seen at Repton how the investigation of a church has become the starting point for a much wider enquiry into the history of the place.

These churches, and many others which have been studied, have some visible features which first provoked their investigation and led to their identification as pre-Conquest. Other churches have proved to have equally long histories, and as much surviving Anglo-Saxon fabric, but it has been more difficult to recognize because the early walls were covered by plaster inside and concrete rendering outside,

FAR RIGHT *Excavation of the interior of the church at Barton-on-Humber by Warwick Rodwell, showing the foundations of a round apse. Like most churches, this one has had many graves cut into the floor, making interpretation of the building sequence more difficult.*

238

Preserved late Saxon
wooden coffin and
skeleton from Barton-
on-Humber. The coffin
seems to have been
held together with
wooden pegs, not iron
nails, so similar coffins
could have vanished
without trace on other
sites.

leaving only much later windows and doors visible to apparently date them. A new approach to investigating churches, which includes removing plaster where possible to examine the stone beneath, was pioneered by Warwick Rodwell at Rivenhall and then at Hadstock, both in Essex. More Anglo-Saxon churches may well be discovered as a result of more such plaster-stripping exercises.

It is even possible to suggest an early origin for buildings where no Anglo-Saxon fabric is visible, and even where none now remains. Hugh Richmond, of the Royal Commission on Historical Monuments, has looked at many churches, recently mostly in Northamptonshire. He has found that buildings can be dated on the basis of elements of their plans just as surely as from architectural detail. The tall narrow naves of Anglo-Saxon churches, with their relatively thin walls, are recognizably different from the lower, thicker walled Norman plans, in the same way that Norman arches are lower and more massive than Anglo-Saxon arches, though both tend to be round. A church with 'Anglo-Saxon' proportions may well contain pre-Conquest fabric. Even if it doesn't, some kind of continuity can be argued, since what has happened is that the original church has been replaced piecemeal over the centuries, so that its original shape has become fossilized in the later versions. Sometimes medieval builders actually built around an old church, reproducing it exactly, only slightly larger, and pulling down the old only when they had finished the new, so the congregation always had some kind of roof over their heads.

One of the churches studied by Hugh Richmond and also by a historian, Mike Franklin, is at King's Sutton in Northamptonshire. Their findings coincide to show that this was an important church before the Conquest. No visible features are earlier than the twelfth century, but the nave has classic early proportions. The walls of the nave are in fact quite probably Anglo-Saxon, with twelfth-century aisles and much later clerestorey windows cut through them. Historically, this was a minster, a large and important church served by a group of priests, and forming the centre of an area equivalent to several parishes. During the Anglo-Saxon period this type of organization gradually gave way to the parochial and diocesan system still in existence, but it is still possible to work out where many of the original minsters were. King's Sutton is also famous for having a large font, used, it is claimed, for the baptism of the alarming St Rumwold, an infant who began preaching almost at birth.

Conclusion

In this book I have looked at the way in which the past has been divided up into slices and interpreted in terms of sudden changes, often explained as the result of the arrival of new peoples. In the first three chapters I looked at prehistoric society in Britain to see if it was always necessary to invoke invaders as an explanation of something new, and I have suggested this was not always the case. The rest of the book deals with invasions which are historically recorded, and shows how much of the previous ways of life did in fact survive each time. It does seem more appropriate to try to think of the past in terms of a continuum with the present, rather than as a series of compartments divided by violent incursions.

The theme of continuity is especially strongly conveyed by the study of the countryside. Even if you look at what seems to be a straightforward medieval site, like Wharram Percy in Yorkshire, a village deserted in the fifteenth century, it turns out that in order to understand it properly you have to follow its history back a very long way.

For more than thirty years John Hurst and Maurice Beresford have been excavating at Wharram Percy every summer. The site of the village is now a deserted green valley except during the digging season, when it is full of people, tents and caravans. The church is still partly standing and there are a couple of cottages occupied until recent years but now in use as site huts. The remains of the medieval village can be seen all along the slopes of the valley, some parts more obvious than others. I remember being shown round years ago by John Hurst, one house-platform after another all clearly visible to him but not always to me. Now there are concrete labels to show where the houses were, but I hope visitors will come on foot still, and that they will not build a road and a car park in the valley.

FAR RIGHT *Aerial view of the deserted medieval village at Wharram Percy, North Yorkshire.*

244

Suggestions for Further Reading

The books listed below include both short and popular books, a few more scholarly works and some catalogues of recent exhibitions. I have tried to include only up-to-date, readable and well-illustrated books in a selection which covers most of the ground I have tried to cover in this book. But it is, of course, only a very small selection of available literature. Visitors to specific monuments will often find books and leaflets on sale, and most museums now have bookstalls. The journal *Current Archaeology* has lively reports on recent excavations.

General Reading

There are a number of good guides to the ancient monuments of Britain and Ireland, many of them now in paperback. Some deal with a part of the country, or with a whole country over time, while others take a specific period or category of sites as their theme. The following are a few which might be most interesting for readers of this book:

Period Guides
MUIR, RICHARD, *The National Trust Guide to Dark Age and Medieval Britain*, George Philip, 1985.
MUIR, RICHARD and WELFARE, HUMPHREY, *The National Trust Guide to Prehistoric and Roman Britain*, George Philip, 1983.

Regional Guides
ASTON, MICHAEL and BURROW, IAN (eds), *The Archaeology of Somerset: A review to 1500 AD*, Somerset County Council, 1982.
HARBISON, PETER, *Guide to the National Monuments in the Republic of Ireland*, Gill and Macmillan, 1970, 2nd ed. 1975.

RITCHIE, ANNA and GRAHAM, *Scotland: Archaeology and Early History*, Thames and Hudson, 1981, paperback 1985.

A book which approaches the history of Britain through its landscape is:
TAYLOR, CHRISTOPHER, *Village and Farmstead*, George Philip, 1983.

1 Hunters and Farmers

COLES, JOHN and ORME, BRYONY, *Prehistory of the Somerset Levels*, Somerset Levels Project, 1982.
RENFREW, A. C., *Before Civilization*, Penguin, 1973.
RENFREW, A. C. (ed.) *The Prehistory of Orkney*, Edinburgh University Press, 1985, Chapters 3 and 4 (A. Ritchie, D. V. Clarke and N. Sharples).

2 The Ritual Landscape

BURL, AUBREY, *Stone Circles of the British Isles*, Yale University Press, 1976.
BURL, AUBREY, *Rites of the Gods*, Dent, 1981.
CHIPPINDALE, CHRISTOPHER, *Stonehenge Revealed*, Thames and Hudson, 1984.
CLARKE, DAVID, COWIE, TREVOR and FOXON, ANDREW, *Symbols of Power at the Time of Stonehenge*, HMSO, 1985.
O'KELLY, MICHAEL, *Newgrange*, Thames and Hudson, 1982.
PITTS, MICHAEL, *Footprints through Avebury*, Stones Print, 1985.

3 A Defended Landscape

COLLIS, JOHN, *The European Iron Age*, Batsford, 1984.
CUNLIFFE, BARRY, *Danebury*, Batsford, 1983.
DYER, JAMES, *Hillforts of England and Wales*, Shire Archaeology, 1981.
REYNOLDS, PETER, *Iron Age Farm: The Butser Experiment*, Colonnade, 1979.
STEAD, I. M., *Celtic Art in Britain before the Roman Conquest*, British Museum, 1985.